CHOOSING
CIVILITY

"The twenty-five simple rules suggested by Forni certainly would go a long way in improving our surroundings."

—Margo Hammond, *St. Petersburg Times*

"This book is the most powerful treatise on the value of kindness that I've ever read. Forget etiquette books that harp on proper fork placement; this book is truly about what matters. After taking a few of P. M. Forni's suggestions to heart, my drive time has become easier, dealing with strangers is more pleasant, and life simply feels terrific. Civility is like a wonderful boomerang: if you send it out, it's bound to come back to you."

—Sujata Massey, author of *The Samurai's Daughter*

"Dr. Forni gently guides the reader to relationship insights that assure love, joy, and meaningful friendship. Anyone interested in living a civil and worthwhile life should read this book."

—Arthur P. Ciaramicoli, Ed.D., Ph.D.,
author of *The Power of Empathy*

"*Choosing Civility* is one of those rare gems one never expected to find but always hoped would appear . . . Forni reclaims manners from the mantelpiece and grounds his advice in the details of everyday life. This book is about how we ought to treat each other. What could be more important than that?"

—Edward Hallowell, M.D., author of *Connect*
and *The Childhood Roots of Adult Happiness*

"Small but mighty new reference . . . the only book I can recommend to all audiences. . . . P. M. Forni deserves great acclaim for developing such potent yet easy to digest remedies for many of today's ills."

—Daniel Buccino, *Metapsychology Online*

CHOOSING CIVILITY

THE TWENTY-FIVE RULES OF CONSIDERATE CONDUCT

P. M. FORNI

ST. MARTIN'S GRIFFIN
NEW YORK

Design by Susan Walsh

Library of Congress Cataloging-in-Publication Data

Forni, P. M.
    Choosing civility : the 25 rules of considerate conduct / P.M.
    Forni.—1st ed.
        p. cm.
    Includes bibliographical references (p. 195).
    ISBN 0-312-28118-8 (hc)
    ISBN 0-312-30250-9 (pbk)
    1. Etiquette.   I. Title.

BJ1853 .F595 2002
395—dc21   2001048651

20 19 18 17

Acknowledgments

Although this is not a long book, I worked at it for several years, at times with absorbing intensity. My first thanks go to the colleagues, students, and friends who gave me the gift of their patience and understanding. Over the years several dedicated assistants took care of the Civility Archive at Johns Hopkins. Strangers, colleagues, and friends discussed civility with me, presented me with their anecdotes, and encouraged me to write. To all of them—too many to mention—my sincere thanks.

Still at the university, President William Brody has been a staunch supporter of my civility-related initiatives, and so has Associate Dean Gary Ostrander. Information Technology Specialists Dean Snyder and Macie Hall showed day after day what crucial assets they are to the university. As I planned and wrote the book, I enjoyed excellent service both in our research library and our campus bookstore. John and Meme Irwin helped during a difficult time, and so did Dr. Daniel McLeod.

Lisa Di Mona made the first call and kept the faith. I feel privileged to be represented by her and her partners at Lark Productions. At St. Martin's Press, George Witte believed in the book from the very beginning. A sterling professional, Marie Estrada made everything easy. My friends in Italy are a constant source of sanity. *Grazie* to all of you, my friends. I owe my greatest debt of gratitude to Virginia, whose love, moral energy, and intelligence continue to be an unmatched positive influence on my life. I dedicate this book to her and all the others who over the years, by giving me their love and affection, made me strive to become a more civil person.

Contents

Foreword

My main goals in this book are to make a persuasive case for making civility a central concern in our lives, and to present and discuss the twenty-five basic rules of civility for our times. I included here all that I think is essential to know about civility not as a philosophical abstraction but as a code of decency to be applied in everyday life. This is a handbook for the practical use of civility.

What is civility? What does it mean to be civil today, at the beginning of the twenty-first century? Is civility in decline? How do we make it part of who we are? What are civility's basic rules? How does civility improve the quality of our lives? How do we practice it among friends, in the workplace, and among strangers? Does it have drawbacks? Are we supposed to be *always* civil? How do we deal with the uncivil? Answering these questions is what this book is about.

That civility is fundamental to the making of a good, successful, and serene life has been for me the most exciting discovery of the last several years. Talking about that discovery is both a privilege and a serious responsibility. It is also a bold move. I wouldn't want to be considered uncivil for presuming to teach civility. The message here is not that I am a flawlessly civil person but that civility is a wonderfully effective tool to enhance the quality of our lives. Seneca voiced the concern that his readers might see a conflict between his lofty teachings and his less-than-perfect conduct. His reply was that he was writing about virtue, not about himself, and that when he condemned vices he first of all condemned his own. Although I try to practice what I preach, my conduct—like Seneca's—is far from perfect. I remain a flawed messenger bearing a good message. As I was writing, my attitude was not one of superiority. I simply wanted to share what seemed to me an exciting insight.

I know that for many of you, reading this book will be at least in part an exercise in covering familiar territory. Such exercises confirm our commitment to the values we hold dear and encourage us to spread the word. In this sense, pondering what we know is as important as gazing upon new vistas. I trust, however, that these pages will give you the thrill of discovery as well. I learned a lot while writing them, and I know that I am not the same person now that I was when I started. For that and for your commitment to listen I am thankful.

Sometimes we read to think, and sometimes to avoid thinking. The second kind of reading entertains us but usually takes us back to the point from which we started—like a midway ride. It leaves us unchallenged and unchanged. The first kind, instead, entails work and fosters growth. For my book, I envision a reader willing to do the work and open to change. When we walk through a house we are tempted to buy, we want to know it in all its details and take the time to absorb its spirit. We run our fingers along the moldings. We touch the walls and the banisters. And we eventually return to and linger in a favorite room. I hope my readers will walk through this book as they would through a house that holds promise.

I urge you to read slowly. Bring the page to life, not only imagining but also internalizing the experience of life that it brings you. To me, the ideal reader is the reader portrayed by the painters of the Renaissance, with a finger in the closed book to mark the page that made him or her stop, meditate, and sometimes look at life in a new, life-changing fashion. As I take leave of these pages, I imagine them in the hands of that reader, hoping that they are worthy of such privilege.

PART ONE

Life and Relationships

WHEREVER THERE IS A HUMAN BEING, THERE IS AN OPPORTU-
NITY FOR A KINDNESS.   —*Lucius Annaeus Seneca*

LOVE IS PATIENT AND KIND; LOVE IS NOT JEALOUS OR BOASTFUL;
IT IS NOT ARROGANT OR RUDE.   —*Paul of Tarsus*

THREE THINGS IN HUMAN LIFE ARE IMPORTANT: THE FIRST IS
TO BE KIND. THE SECOND IS TO BE KIND. AND THE THIRD IS
TO BE KIND.   —*Henry James*

Here we are at the end of the century, drifting through a
heroless age. We have no leaders we can trust, no visions to
invest in, no faith to ride. All we have are our own protean
moralities, our countless private codes, which we each shape
and reshape according to our own selfish needs. We don't
dare to think too far ahead, we can't see too far ahead. Here
we are, trapped by whatever season we find ourselves enduring, waiting out the weather, staring at a drought sun, stu-
pefied, helpless—or scrambling like fools to make it home
before the rain really comes down and the dry river floods
and the hills crash into the valley. Where do we find the
courage to do what is right?

I came across this passage by novelist Peter Gadol when everybody
was getting ready to celebrate the turn of both the century and
the millennium. It was a striking description of a malaise with

which, to a greater or a lesser extent, many of us were familiar. Gadol's words resonated with me in particular because of my involvement with the Johns Hopkins Civility Project, a cluster of academic and outreach activities aimed at assessing the relevance of civility and good manners in today's society. While working on the Project, I had been giving thought to the widely perceived decline in the quality of social interaction—the so-called coarsening of America.

Gadol's words on the end of the twentieth century apply to the beginning of the new century as well. Constant uncertainty about our identities and our future seems at times our only certainty. Long-established values appear obsolete, but to agree on what the new ones should be is a daunting task. Quite often we don't know where to look for standards against which to measure our efforts to be good citizens of the world. In fact, the notion of standards itself has been growing more and more problematic.

And yet we still need to be able to say yes to some things and no to others as a matter of principle and with enough conviction. We still need to believe in something that will give us our vital daily dose of meaning and motivation. As we grapple with the complexities of our age, I suggest in this book that we agree on one principle: that a crucial measure of our success in life is the way we treat one another every day of our lives.

> THEN [GOOD MANNERS] MUST BE INSPIRED BY THE GOOD HEART. THERE IS NO BEAUTIFIER OF COMPLEXION, OR FORM, OR BEHAVIOR, LIKE THE WISH TO SCATTER JOY AND NOT PAIN AROUND US. —*Ralph Waldo Emerson*

When we lessen the burden of living for those around us we are doing well; when we add to the misery of the world we are not. To me, this is a simple, practical philosophy that makes sense and feels right. And since I started speaking in public on these issues several years ago, I have discovered that it makes sense and feels right to people from every walk of life and every part of the world. How are we to carry out the business of living day in and day out in accordance with this premise? I propose that as a society we take a new, close look at that intriguing code of behavior based on respect, restraint, and responsibility that we call civility.

M. Scott Peck chose to open his wise guidebook to smart, decent, and loving living with an utterly plain and clear statement. "Life is difficult" is the founding truth of his work, one he connects to "Life is suffering," the first of the Four Noble Truths taught by Buddha. Of course, countless versions of this truth appear in wisdom literature throughout history. "Life is difficult." I like the simplicity of the utterance. We can all benefit from basic truths stated in direct and simple language. In the hasty confusion of our days, we easily lose sight of basic truths. As we fail to make them part of our everyday thinking, we eventually become unable to recognize them clearly and confront them effectively. And so we stumble through life in a cloud of dust raised by our own misguided steps.

When we manage to make real contact with a basic truth, sometimes we are inspired to act upon it, and thus we may change our lives radically and permanently. Greatness is not just in the truth itself but in what we can do with it. "Once we truly know that life is difficult—once we truly understand and accept it—then life is no longer difficult," says M. Scott Peck. Now, we may be able to reach this wisdom and strength or we may not. All of us, however, can find ways to cope effectively with difficulty.

That life is difficult is the founding truth of any book that offers practical help. Millions of pages would not have been written if life were not difficult and we didn't need help coping with its challenges. The message that we want to hear—that we never tire of hearing—is that although life is difficult, it is not unbearable; that there is something relatively simple that we can do to overcome life's difficulty. We are not passive vessels into which pain, anxiety, and sorrow are poured. In fact, we can become effective managers of our actions and emotions. As such, we can reduce the impact of sorrow and unhappiness upon our lives. Although life entails hardship and suffering, we can do something about it—we can always do something about it. Life may be difficult, but serenity, contentment, well-being, and even happiness are not only possible but also within relatively easy reach.

I am convinced that, to a significant extent, life is what our relationships make it. Every page of this book is imbued with this simple conviction. Good relationships make our lives good; bad relationships make our lives bad. We are usually happy (or unhappy) with others. Although at times we can be happy in spite of others, we are usually happy thanks to them, thanks to the good relationships we have with them. To learn how to be happy we must learn how to live well with others, and civility is a key to that. Through civility we develop thoughtfulness, foster effective self-expression and communication, and widen the range of our benign responses. Civility allows us to connect successfully with others. While there is no substitute for healthy self-esteem, we also need to transcend our Selves. Finding a comfortable balance between the two is where everyday wellness and happiness begin, and what civility is all about.

We exist and we perceive our identity not in a vacuum but rather in relation to others. Life is relational. Whether we like it or not, we are wax upon which others leave their mark. When someone sees us as a thing to use or abuse, that becomes part of who we are in our own eyes as well (self-esteem notwithstanding). When we are on the receiving end of an act of kindness, we feel validated. We translate that act into a very simple, very powerful unspoken message to ourselves: I am not alone, I have value and my life has meaning.

What Is Civility?

MAYBE I WAS COMING DOWN WITH CHANGE-OF-SEASON INFLU-
ENZA. IF SO, I SHOULD REALLY CONSIDER BUYING A LITTLE
WHITE HALF MASK FOR MY SUBWAY RIDE HOME.

—*Sujata Massey*

For many years literature was my life. I spent most of my time reading, teaching, and writing on Italian fiction and poetry. One day, while lecturing on the *Divine Comedy,* I looked at my students and realized that I wanted them to be kind human beings more than I wanted them to know about Dante. I told them that if they knew everything about Dante and then they went out and treated an elderly lady on the bus unkindly, I'd feel that I had failed as a teacher. I have given dozens of lectures and workshops on civility in the last few years, and I have derived much satisfaction from addressing audiences I could not have reached speaking on litera-ture. I know, however, that reading literature can develop the kind of imagination without which civility is impossible. To be fully human we must be able to imagine others' hurt and to relate it to the hurt we would experience if we were in their place. Con-sideration is imagination on a moral track.

Sometimes the participants in my workshops write on a sheet of paper what civility means to them. In no particular order, here are a number of key civility-related notions I have collected over the years from those sheets:

Respect for others	Community service
Care	Tact
Consideration	Equality
Courtesy	Sincerity
Golden rule	Morality
Respect of others' feelings	Honesty
Niceness	Awareness
Politeness	Trustworthiness
Respect of others' opinions	Friendship
Maturity	Table manners
Kindness	Moderation
Manners	Listening
Being accommodating	Compassion
Fairness	Being agreeable
Decency	Going out of one's way
Self-control	Friendliness
Concern	Lending a hand
Justice	Propriety
Tolerance	Abiding by rules
Selflessness	Good citizenship
Etiquette	Peace

This list tells us that

• Civility is complex.

• Civility is good.

- Whatever civility might be, it has to do with courtesy, politeness, and good manners.

- Civility belongs in the realm of ethics.

These four points have guided me in writing this book. Like my workshop participants, I am inclusive rather than exclusive in defining civility. Courtesy, politeness, manners, and civility are all, in essence, forms of awareness. Being civil means being constantly aware of others and weaving restraint, respect, and consideration into the very fabric of this awareness. Civility is a form of goodness; it is gracious goodness. But it is not just an attitude of benevolent and thoughtful relating to other individuals; it also entails an active interest in the well-being of our communities and even a concern for the health of the planet on which we live.

Saying "please" and "thank you"; lowering our voice whenever it may threaten or interfere with others' tranquillity; raising funds for a neighborhood renovation program; acknowledging a newcomer to the conversation; welcoming a new neighbor; listening to understand and help; respecting those different from us; responding with restraint to a challenge; properly disposing of a piece of trash left by someone else; properly disposing of dangerous industrial pollutants; acknowledging our mistakes; refusing to participate in malicious gossip; making a new pot of coffee for the office machine after drinking the last cup; signaling our turns when driving; yielding our seat on a bus whenever it seems appropriate; alerting the person sitting behind us on a plane when we are about to lower the back of our seat; standing close to the right-side handrail on an escalator; stopping to give directions to someone who is lost; stopping at red lights; disagreeing with poise; yielding with grace when losing an argument, these diverse behaviors are all imbued with the spirit of civility.

Civility, courtesy, politeness, and *manners* are not perfect synonyms, as etymology clearly shows.

> IN LIFE COURTESY AND SELF-POSSESSION, AND IN THE ARTS STYLE, ARE THE SENSIBLE IMPRESSIONS OF THE FREE MIND, FOR BOTH ARISE OUT OF A DELIBERATE SHAPING OF ALL THINGS, AND FROM NEVER BEING SWEPT AWAY, WHATEVER THE EMOTION, INTO CONFUSION OR DULLNESS.
> —*William Butler Yeats*

Courtesy is connected to *court* and evoked in the past the superior qualities of character and bearing expected in those close to royalty. Etymologically, when we are courteous we are courtierlike. Although today we seldom make this connection, courtesy still suggests excellence and elegance in bestowing respect and attention. It can also suggest deference and formality.

> THE VERY ESSENCE OF POLITENESS SEEMS TO BE TO TAKE CARE THAT BY OUR WORDS AND ACTIONS WE MAKE OTHER PEOPLE PLEASED WITH US AS WELL AS WITH THEMSELVES.
> —*Jean de La Bruyère*

To understand *politeness,* we must think of *polish.* The polite are those who have polished their behavior. They have put some effort into bettering themselves, but they are sometimes looked upon with suspicion. Expressions such as "polite reply," "polite lie," and "polite applause" connect politeness to hypocrisy. It is true that the polite are inclined to veil their own feelings to spare someone else's. Self-serving lying, however, is always beyond the pale of politeness. If politeness is a quality of character (alongside courtesy, good manners, and civility), it cannot become a flaw. A suave manipulator may appear to be polite but is not.

> THERE IS ALWAYS A BEST WAY OF DOING EVERYTHING, IF IT BE TO BOIL AN EGG. MANNERS ARE THE HAPPY WAY OF DOING THINGS; EACH ONCE A STROKE OF GENIUS OR OF LOVE, NOW REPEATED AND HARDENED INTO USAGE.
> —*Ralph Waldo Emerson*

When we think of good *manners* we often think of children being taught to say "please" and "thank you" and chew with their mouths closed. This may prevent us from looking at manners with the attention they deserve. *Manner* comes from *manus,* the Latin word for "hand." *Manner* and *manners* have to do with the use of our hands. A manner is the way something is done, a mode of handling. Thus *manners* came to refer to behavior in social interaction—the way we handle the encounter between Self and Other. We have good manners when we use our hands well—when we handle others with care. When we rediscover the connection of *manner* with *hand,* the hand that, depending on our will and sensitivity, can strike or lift, hurt or soothe, destroy or heal, we understand the importance—for children and adults alike—of having good manners.

> BEING CIVIL TO ONE ANOTHER IS MUCH MORE ACTIVE AND POSITIVE A GOOD THAN MERE POLITENESS OR COURTESY, BUT LIKE MANY OTHER IMPORTANT GOODS, SUCH AS GENEROSITY, GRATITUDE, OR SOLIDARITY, IT IS NOT THE SORT OF THING THAT CAN BE "DEMANDED" AS A MATTER OF DUTY, LIKE A MORAL ENTITLEMENT. —*Robert B. Pippin*

Civility's defining characteristic is its ties to *city* and *society*. The word derives from the Latin *civitas*, which means "city," especially in the sense of civic community. *Civitas* is the same word from which *civilization* comes. The age-old assumption behind civility is that life in the city has a civilizing effect. The city is where we enlighten our intellect and refine our social skills. And as we are shaped by the city, we learn to give of ourselves for the sake of the city. Although we can describe the civil as courteous, polite, and well mannered, etymology reminds us that they are also supposed to be good citizens and good neighbors.

Respect in Action

Living according to the principle of respect for persons is difficult. And yet we can do it, thanks in part to our ability to identify with others and—at least to a certain extent—to feel what they feel. This ability is empathy.

> EMPATHY SHINES ITS LIGHT ON OUR DEEPEST NEEDS, NEVER ALLOWING US TO FORGET THAT OUR VERY SURVIVAL DE-PENDS ON OUR ABILITY TO ACCURATELY UNDERSTAND AND SENSITIVELY RESPOND TO EACH OTHER.
> —*Arthur P. Ciaramicoli and Katherine Ketcham*

The extraordinary relevance of the rules of civility to our lives is that by following them we put into everyday practice the principle of respect for persons. Civility does the work of empathy.

With a training in civility we develop the invaluable habit of considering that no action of ours is without consequences for others and anticipating what those consequences will be. We learn to act in a responsible and caring way. Choosing civility means choosing to do the right thing for others—for the "city." The by-product of doing justice to others is the enrichment of our own lives. I hope that we will never tire of rediscovering that being kind is good for the kind.

Yes, we live in an age of radical individualism and cultural relativism. Yes, the lack of meaningful coherence in our lives can be disheartening. And yes, sometimes we feel lost because of the dizzying amount and variety of information readily available in a world enveloped by the uninterrupted buzz of the electronic media. But we need not succumb to bafflement, indifference, or despair. "Our countless private codes which we each shape and reshape according to our own selfish needs," to use Peter Gadol's words, are far from being our only viable reference for conducting the business of living. We needn't "scramble like fools." One thing we can do is act upon the realization that the quality of our lives depends upon our ability to relate and connect. Harmonious and caring relationships foster a happy life. In order to build such relationships, we need the respect, consideration, and kindness that we easily grant to and receive from our fellow humans when we are civil.

Happiness and the Mind

THE HAPPINESS OF YOUR LIFE DEPENDS UPON THE QUALITY OF
YOUR THOUGHTS.   *—Marcus Aurelius*

HAPPINESS DOES NOT DEPEND ON OUTWARD THINGS, BUT ON
THE WAY WE SEE THEM.   *—Leo Tolstoy*

The Bible, Gautama Buddha, Marcus Aurelius, Ralph Waldo
Emerson, and William James are among the most frequently
quoted sources of this momentous notion: our happiness does not
spring from the events of our lives but rather from how we choose
to respond to those events. Many students of human happiness see
life satisfaction as a product of the thinking Self.

Our lives are made of events over which we have little or no
control. What we *can* control is how we are going to think about
those events. Although we cannot choose no traffic over congested
highways for our back-to-work Monday-morning commute, we can
choose how to react to traffic. Even in the worst of circumstances,
we can react with positive thoughts. While stuck on a beltway in
our motorized metal cocoons we can think that this is a good
opportunity to do some serious, undisturbed work-related planning. Such a positive reaction to a nonpositive event will yield
happy feelings rather than unhappy ones.

Our feelings are the products of our thoughts. A positive thought produces a feeling of contentment or happiness, a negative one a feeling of sadness or despondency. If we have control over what we *think* about what happens to us, we have control over how we *feel* about it as well. This means, in turn, that we can be the makers of our own happiness. To say that this is an empowering message is an understatement. It comes, however, with quite a burden of personal responsibility, since it prevents us from blaming our misery on our circumstances. Be that as it may, the pronouncement of a thousand thinkers is unequivocal: our contentment and happiness are a matter of personal attitude.

HE WHO HAS SUCH LITTLE KNOWLEDGE OF HUMAN VALUE AS TO SEEK HAPPINESS BY CHANGING ANYTHING BUT HIS DISPOSITION WILL WASTE HIS LIFE IN FRUITLESS EFFORTS AND MULTIPLY THE GRIEF HE PROPOSES TO REMOVE.
—*Samuel Johnson*

Who wouldn't want to acquire an attitude that invites happiness into our lives? Unfortunately, having a positive attitude is not as simple as putting on new clothes. I think that we should take the invitation to self-reliance with a modicum of common sense. To say that we are to look inside ourselves for ways to cope successfully with the difficulties of life doesn't mean that we should ignore the outside world. Our relationships with others are an invaluable resource of meaning and happiness.

THERE IS NO JOY EXCEPT IN HUMAN RELATIONSHIPS.
—*Antoine de Saint-Exupéry*

When we excel in the art of sustaining good relationships we can afford to be less than perfect in the art of a positive attitude. And contentment and joy will come to us in unalloyed form.

How Do We Learn to Love?

Of course, human relationships are not always joyful. Sigmund Freud saw the quest for happiness as central to the human experience. What do human beings want? They "want to become happy and to remain so" was his famous answer. He went on to list the threats to this program of pleasure. Suffering can come from our sickness-prone bodies and from the destructive forces of nature. But the single most painful source of unhappiness, he observed, is perhaps our relationships with others.

Others inevitably limit our individual gratification. If there are two of us and only one apple, I may feel I should give you half of it even if I'd rather eat it all. Or you may take my apple from me. In this sense, the happiness of others is where our happiness ends. However, we also perceive others as a source of happiness. Giving you half of my apple may in fact give me more pleasure than eating the whole apple. Keeping away from others to avoid getting hurt just won't do. Our challenge is to pursue relationships while keeping at a minimum the hurt that they entail. How can we do that?

When confronting a hurtful event, we can try to activate our internal discipline. We can apply our positive attitude. Here I am more interested in what we can do to prevent hurtful events from happening in the first place. Although we do not have total control over the events that affect our lives, we do have some. We can make it so that certain events will be more likely to occur than others. There is a proven way to keep the hurt that comes from relationships to a minimum, and that is by training ourselves to become good at being with others. How to acquire this invaluable behavioral literacy is not a mystery. A training in civility is part of our basic training as social beings. Civility is the preventive medicine we need.

"Forget love. Try good manners," is the parting shot in a barbed letter that Siddalee, the protagonist of Rebecca Wells's novel *Divine Secrets of the Ya-Ya Sisterhood,* receives from her mother, Vivi. Since nobody really knows how to love, says Vivi, we must, at least, be nice to one another. I find Vivi's utterance striking, even though I disagree with the bleak assessment behind it. We often do know how to love. We know how to love when we have developed a sensitivity to the feelings and needs of others. The problem is not that humans are by nature incapable of knowing how to love, but that the circumstances of their lives often prevent them from learning.

I am optimistic about our ability to better ourselves. We can learn to be decent and caring; we can learn to give of ourselves; we can learn to love. How do we do that? The same way we learn how to speak, read, swim, or ride a bicycle: we need somebody to teach us, and we need practice. The reason I like Vivi's advice is that I read it as saying that love is a point of arrival, a goal difficult to achieve, and before we think we can love we need basic training. First things first. First we discipline our ego to look beyond the narrow confines of its immediate needs; then we will have a chance to understand what real love is. First manners, then love. After the training there will be those who are able to love others, even strangers, as they love themselves. And there will be those whose love will be confined to their friends and family. All, however, will have learned to practice respect, restraint, concern, and benevolence to some degree. Manners are the first steps of the soul toward love.

Civility and Self-Expression

EMOTIONAL SELF-CONTROL IS NOT THE SAME AS OVERCONTROL, THE STIFLING OF ALL FEELING AND SPONTANEITY. . . . WHEN SUCH EMOTIONAL SUPPRESSION IS CHRONIC, IT CAN IMPAIR THINKING, HAMPER INTELLECTUAL PERFORMANCE AND INTERFERE WITH SMOOTH SOCIAL INTERACTION. BY CONTRAST, EMOTIONAL COMPETENCE IMPLIES WE HAVE A CHOICE AS TO HOW WE EXPRESS OUR FEELINGS. *—Daniel Goleman*

RESTRAINT OFFERS A SPACE BETWEEN INTENTION AND ACTION AND THE OPPORTUNITY TO PROTECT OTHERS FROM ACTIONS OR REACTIONS THAT SHOULD EXIST ONLY IN YOUR IMAGINATION. *—Stephanie Dowrick*

Does civility impose restrictions on our everyday behavior? Of course it does. Does this mean that when we are civil we necessarily give up self-expression? No, it does not. Is civility a hindrance to our quest for a good life? It doesn't have to be, when it's practiced in a healthy way. In fact, the opposite is true. Civility is crucial to the achievement of a well-balanced and happy life.

- Sometimes we confuse having fun with being happy. The latter is virtually impossible without a personal history of restraint and discipline. Sometimes in order to reach happiness we must forgo fun.

- Civility is liberating. It frees us from slavery to self-absorption, impulse, and mood.

- Sometimes we confuse self-possession with self-denial. Civility's restraint has to do with the former, not the latter.

Self-expression belongs to the natural order of things. Indeed, we owe it to ourselves to express ourselves. There is something good and healthful in bringing forward and acting upon our thoughts and feelings. However, this doesn't mean that all we may want to express is equally worthy of expression. The unruly, the brazen, and the reckless give self-expression a bad name. Going through life under the sway of unchecked impulses may count as self-expression, but it is irresponsible self-indulgence—and painful collisions are sure to ensue. Self-expression at its best is instead a happy medium between self-effacement and self-indulgence.

RUDENESS IS THE WEAK MAN'S IMITATION OF STRENGTH.
—*Eric Hoffer*

In any given circumstance of life we have the alternative of stopping and thinking before acting—the alternative of restraint. Restraint is our inner designated driver. We all have it, and we all can learn to summon it whenever we need it. Instead of unthinkingly rushing into action, we can ask ourselves:

- Do I really want to do this?

- Is anybody going to be hurt by this?

- Will I like having done this?

This allows us to make sound decisions. We are stuck in traffic, but we decide against rolling ahead of others down the emergency lane; we are incensed by a salesclerk's arrogant attitude, but we manage to remain both calm and assertive; although another car slips into our parking spot, we refuse to start the seemingly obligatory shouting match; we are exhausted after a long day, but we still listen patiently to our friend's seemingly endless carping.

Restraint is an infusion of thinking—and thoughtfulness—into everything we do. We choose the behavior that, although it may not seem the most gratifying now, will make us feel good five minutes from now, tomorrow, or next year. Restraint is the art of feeling good later. In fact, most of life's wisdom is about choosing what will make us feel good later.

While traveling by train in Italy, my wife, Virginia, and I found ourselves in the boisterous company of high school students on a day trip. I said nothing for ten uncomfortable minutes, hoping that they would settle down. Not a chance. Their continued disregard for the presence of others certainly fell short of charming, but what brought me close to an angry outburst was the acquiescence of their teachers. For a moment I felt like lashing out at both students and teachers. I knew immediately, though, that I wouldn't do so. I knew that later I wouldn't like having done it.

I made a conscious effort to remain clearheaded. Then, speaking in a quiet but firm tone, I asked the two students in the seats across the aisle to be so kind as to lower their voices so that I could have a conversation with Virginia. Rather than chastising them, I made them aware of my need. I informed them, but I made it clear that with the information came their responsibility to do something about it. Other students and the teachers overheard me. There was some nervous laughter and a few mockingly accentuated hushing noises. But there was also a general change in behavior. The remainder of the trip was substantially quieter, and when we reached Rome we all said good-bye, wishing one another a pleasant visit.

It was restraint that made possible the satisfactory resolution of the incident. My restraint, and also the students'. Some may say that by being civil to each other we stifled our self-expression. But we can also say that we chose to express one part of ourselves rather than another. Although it may appear that we give up self-expression when we exercise it, in truth restraint can be as much an expression of our Selves as is unfettered behavior. Yes, practicing civility may limit our immediate gratification. That's why we are tempted to be rude. But civility at its best is not a threat to life fulfillment. Contentment does not reside in what civility tells us we shouldn't say or shouldn't do. Rather, contentment is, to a large extent, the result of many good choices we make as we interact with others. Civility assists us in making choices that increase the quality of our lives.

As a society we have done a good job of encouraging self-esteem, but not as good a job of teaching self-control. We all need self-esteem. Self-esteem is good, it keeps us sane, it is an immune system for our souls. However, when we are too focused on raising self-esteem, we swell the ranks of the self-absorbed. Many youngsters who have been fed supersized portions of self-esteem have trouble transcending their own immediate concerns, needs, and desires. Therefore they are not attentive, considerate, courteous, and kind. They are trapped in a narcissistic cage we have built for them. Whenever this happens, hurt is bound to ensue.

Nice Guys Finish Last.
Or Do They?

❧❧

WE HEAR OF A FUTURE WHERE RELATIONSHIPS ARE KEY AND
PEOPLE ARE VALUED, WHERE NOT JUST THE TASK WELL PER-
FORMED BUT THE LIFE WELL LIVED IS WHAT COUNTS.
—*Frances Hesselbein*

Many people see no place for civility in a less-than-perfect world.
They believe that in our aggressive and competitive society civility
is a luxury they can't afford. If you are polite you are perceived as
weak and you are brushed aside, they say. Being considerate and
kind is hazardous to your self-esteem, professional ambitions, and
net worth. So: check your sensitivity at the door, roll up your
sleeves, don't pull any punches, and collect your prize.

It is not my intention to dismiss such an attitude. Can you
achieve substantial results with it? Indeed you can, especially in
the short run. The question is: do you want to win that way and
can you see yourself winning that way?

Nice guys don't have to finish last. Not if they are also smart,
imaginative, dedicated, and persevering. Niceness works as part of
a winning combination. This is one of the few certainties on which
we can rely when it comes to choosing our values and shaping our
attitudes in both the personal and professional arenas.

When I think of the nice/civil person of the new century, I recall a passage by E. M. Forster, contained in his essay "What I Believe":

> I believe in aristocracy . . . if that is the right word, and if a democrat may use it. Not an aristocracy of power, based upon rank and influence, but an aristocracy of the sensitive, the considerate and the plucky. Its members are to be found in all nations and all classes, and all through the ages, and there is a secret understanding between them when they meet. They represent the true human tradition, the one permanent victory of our queer race over cruelty and chaos. Thousands of them perish in obscurity, a few are great names. They are sensitive for others, as for themselves, they are considerate without being fussy, their pluck is not swankiness but the power to endure, and they can take a joke.

"Sensitive," "considerate," but also "plucky." Forster encourages us to be civil without self-effacement, to be sensitive and assertive at the same time, to practice respect for others as an extension of our self-respect, and to do all this with seriousness of intent and lightness of touch. To speak of pluck and the power to endure in the same breath with sensitivity and consideration; to speak of kindness as a kind of strength: this is quite a lesson. We may want to keep it in mind as we face the new century deciding what our next steps are going to be.

To be civil—to behave, that is, in a manner that takes into consideration the feelings and the comfort of others—means practicing the art of giving. This practice is at the same time free and binding. Although not obligatory (it is not prescribed by law), it creates a bond between those involved. When we are courteous, we expect to be answered in kind. Even a minimal transcending of the Self calls for a comparable transcending on the part of the

Other. By treating you the best way I know how, I appeal to the best in you, urging you to do the same. The practice of civility is the applying of gentle force with the goal that everybody be a winner in the delicate game of the social exchange.

As an art, civility has rules one can learn and facility with these rules can improve with practice. This is the good news. The bad news is that often we are unable to imagine the benefits of that learning and practice. We thus leave untapped a resource that would prove invaluable in increasing the quality of our lives. This book is about the benefits of civility and the best ways to make them part of our everyday lives.

The Science of Love
and Social Support

WHEN YOU FEEL LOVED, NURTURED, CARED FOR, SUPPORTED, AND INTIMATE, YOU ARE MUCH MORE LIKELY TO BE HAPPIER AND HEALTHIER. YOU HAVE A MUCH LOWER RISK OF GETTING SICK AND, IF YOU DO, A MUCH GREATER CHANCE OF SURVIVING. —*Dean Ornish*

SOCIAL TIES ARE THE CHEAPEST MEDICINE WE HAVE.
—*Shelley E. Taylor*

- Healthy young men from two Harvard classes of the early 1950s were asked to fill out a questionnaire that would assess how close they were to their parents. A check of their medical records 35 years later yielded intriguing data. One hundred percent of the men who had reported low levels of closeness to both parents had been diagnosed in the following years with serious diseases such as heart disease and duodenal ulcer. Among those who had reported good, warm relationships with both parents only 47 percent had been similarly diagnosed.

- In 1965 Lisa Berkman—a pioneer in the field of mind-body medicine—and her colleagues recorded the social ties (marital status, friendships, church affiliation, etc.) of several thousand men and women from Alameda County, California. Nine years later, in 1979, the researchers set out to assess the study participants' health. They found that the people living in isolation were dying at a rate 1.9 to 3.1 times higher than the people well integrated in their social environments. In the years following 1979, several other studies confirmed that lack of social connection presents a serious health risk.

- In the 1990s, Dr. Sheldon Cohen of Carnegie Mellon University and his collaborators assessed the extent of social connections of 276 healthy volunteers aged 18 to 55. Then they gave their subjects nasal drops containing one of two rhinoviruses, with the goal to monitor the insurgence of the common cold. The researchers found that, regardless of the virus they were given, the subjects who were part of diverse social networks were more effective in fighting off the cold. Those with six or more types of social ties fared four times better than those with one to three types.

- Dr. Janice Kiecolt-Glaser and her team at Ohio State University showed that separated and divorced men were not as healthy as married men. They also showed that men whose married lives were of poor quality had less effective immune systems. Hostility between husband and wife is certainly bad for their health. In another study, Drs. Kiecolt-Glaser and Ronald Glaser focused on couples who had been married for several decades. They found that the immune systems of couples who argued a lot were weaker than those of couples who didn't. A review of dozens of studies has shown that hostility as a personality trait is a major risk factor in the development of coronary heart disease.

In order to be healthy, we need to live among others. Since social integration is healthful, social skills—the skills that make social integration possible—are utterly relevant to our health. When we are skilled in managing our relationships, we are more likely to build and maintain a network of support. Far from being just a matter of good form, civility is also a matter of good health. Quite simply: being good is good for you. To stay healthy we need to perceive our lives as having purpose and meaning. We usually find purpose and meaning linked to the presence of others in our lives. All the more important, then, that we learn how to treat them fairly, respectfully, and considerately. As we do, it becomes clearer and clearer that civility is the place of encounter between Self and Other where altruism and self-interest find a harmonious way to coexist.

Having relational competence is of great advantage to those of us in the second part of our lives. When we retire we are at risk of finding ourselves isolated. During our working years many people *have* to be around us who would *prefer* not to. But when business is not a factor anymore, those people have no incentive to remain part of our lives. If we are kind and considerate, people will *want* to be around us, and we benefit from enduring circles of attention and care.

About the Rules

Rules of civility have been around in one form or another for a very long time. They appear in the texts of all religions, from Judaism and Christianity to Confucianism, from Islam to Hinduism. They can be found in Renaissance tracts on the ideal gentleman and gentlewoman, in Victorian books of manners, and in the works of philosophers from Plato to Kant. Today's self-help manuals on social skills try to keep these rules alive, as do the pamphlets by civil society supporters of all stripes.

> WE HAVE A CHOICE ABOUT HOW WE BEHAVE, AND THAT MEANS WE HAVE THE CHOICE TO OPT FOR CIVILITY AND GRACE. —*Dwight Currie*

I have tried to condense that vast body of work and its wisdom into 25 essential rules. Although the rules of civility you will find here have withstood the test of time, I have reconfigured and re-written them with the needs of our time in mind, drawing on my personal experience. Following them may not feel like a shortcut to a good life. If anything, these rules may feel like a "longcut," since civility requires work and dedication. But they do offer a path to serenity and contentment.

PART TWO

The Rules

1. Pay Attention

A HUMAN MOMENT OCCURS ANYTIME TWO OR MORE PEOPLE ARE TOGETHER, PAYING ATTENTION TO ONE ANOTHER.
—Edward M. Hallowell

THE PRINCIPAL FORM THAT THE WORK OF LOVE TAKES IS ATTENTION.
—M. Scott Peck

Several middle schoolers are walking down the hall. They are laughing, they are teasing one another, and they are loud. As they walk by a closed classroom door, one of them does the unexpected. Only a few seconds ago she seemed oblivious to anything but the microcosm of her giggling peers. But now, as she glances at the closed door, the thought that a class or an exam may be taking place behind it flashes through her mind. Immediately she lowers her voice and hastens to hush her friends.

A small act? Yes, but an impressive one nonetheless. First, the young woman managed to see in her mind's eye what may have been happening beyond the closed door; then, she was able to imagine the discomfort that her group's noisemaking could cause; finally, she was willing to act upon her empathic imagination. This complex process, however, could not have started had she not been aware of her surroundings. She could be considerate because *she was paying attention*.

Without attention, no meaningful interaction is possible. Our first responsibility, when we are with others, is to pay attention, *to attend to*. Etymology tells us that attention has to do with "turning toward," "extending toward," "stretching." Thus attention is a tension connecting us to the world around us. Only after we *notice* the world can we begin to *care* for it. Every act of kindness is, first of all, an act of attention. We may see a coworker in need of a word of encouragement, but it is only if we pay attention that we may do something about it. We may hear a child cry, but again, our help is contingent upon our stopping and taking notice.

We spend much of our daily lives neglecting to pay attention. I know I often go through my surroundings without taking them in, without making them mine. When I drive from home to the office and back along my well-traveled route, rarely is my attention struck by the individual objects of the world around me. Rather, my glance is trapped by the patina of the familiar covering them. A tree is nothing but a tree, a storefront just another storefront, a bus just a bus, a passerby just a passerby. Nothing interesting there.

I believe we are all familiar with this kind of experience, just as we are acquainted with its opposite. We also are able to relate to the world as a new and interesting place, as something worthy of attention. Sometimes we need a special occasion to do so. Now I am covering the same stretch of road I cover every day, but this time a friend visiting from out of town is with me. As I point out the sights to him, my perception becomes keener and the familiar turns slightly unfamiliar. I manage to see what I see every day as if for the first time. The tree becomes an old dogwood. A handsome calico cat sleeps in the storefront's window. The bus roaring by flashes a destination that reminds me of a resort I loved as a child. And the passerby is a middle-aged, seemingly upset woman pressing a white handkerchief to her mouth. What have I been doing? I have been looking at my everyday world through the eyes of the stranger. I have stripped reality of its generic wrapper. I have been paying attention.

When we relate to the world as if we were on automatic pilot, we can hardly be at our best in our encounters with our fellow human beings. When we pay attention, when we are alert to the world, we improve substantially the quality of our responses and therefore the quality of our lives and of the lives of those who touch ours. We want to inhabit every situation with ease but at the same time maintain a little bit of the stranger's ability to be "impressed" by reality. We want to allow reality to leave its mark upon our consciousness:

- I am not *just* talking with *a* colleague but with *this* colleague, who told me several weeks ago that he was concerned about his child's health and whom I have seen grow more and more preoccupied in the last few days. I will keep this in mind as we plan our next month's teamwork.

- I am not *just* reminiscing with *a* high school friend but with *this* friend, who married early, never went to college, and seems threatened by the friendships I developed in college. I should reassure her of my commitment to *our* friendship.

- I am not *just* critiquing the work of *a* student. I am speaking to *this* individual student, whom I saw struggling during the semester as she tried to match the performances of more seasoned fellow students. As I go over her essay with her, I will remind her of her strengths and tell her I believe in her potential.

- A car is trying to join the traffic flow from the parking lot to my right. Since the traffic is bumper-to-bumper, if everybody thinks of that car as *just* another car, its driver will be stuck forever. I will slow down to let him in ahead of me.

- Virginia notices that in the back of our train car several of the travelers are reading and working. Since we want to talk, she observes, it would be a good idea to sit in front, in order to disturb them as little as possible with our chatter.

Attention is what all these situations have in common—or, to be more precise, the victory of attention over carelessness, indifference, and inertia. When we slow down the pace of attention we do justice to life by taking it seriously. When we pay attention we do justice to the presence of others in our lives. Attention entails a transcending of the Self. Through it we confer value upon the lives of others. When I show you that you are worthy of my attention, I am acknowledging and honoring your worth.

Although attention is a reading of what is around us, it is also timely self-awareness. We want to be aware of how we are reacting to the circumstances at the very time we are reacting to them. We want to make sure that there is a good fit between how we feel and what we do. Somebody's words hurt us and we perceive a swell of outrage inside. Let's stop for a moment to pay attention to it. Is it warranted? Are we overreacting? Are we about to respond in a way we will soon regret? As a friend asks us to recommend him for a job, our first reaction is one of uneasiness. Before we do anything else it's a good idea to pay attention to why we feel that way. Is it because we honestly believe he is not a good candidate for the job? Is it because we resent his good opportunity? Is it a mixture of the two?

Attention looks two ways: outward and inward. As it checks

the world, it checks our souls. It is up to us to put to good use its inexhaustible wealth of information. When we manage to do that, we are at our best and live life to the fullest.

SALT AND PEPPER

When I teach my courses on civility and manners, I tell my students: "We are eating together in the university cafeteria and I ask you to pass me the salt. What do you do?"

The exchange that follows that question usually goes like this:

"I will pass you the salt," answers student A, somewhat puzzled by having to state the obvious.

"What else?" I press.

"That's it," he replies. "You asked for the salt and I'll pass you the salt."

"What else?" I insist.

Fifteen seconds of silence, then a tentative answer comes from student B: "I will pass you the pepper as well?"

"Yes," I reply. "That's what we find in books of etiquette: salt and pepper always travel together. The books, however, neglect to tell us why. You tell me, then, the reasons behind the rule."

Student B is ready now: "I will give you the pepper as well because you may need it later?"

That's indeed part of the rationale. And that's where ethics intersects etiquette. "You," I tell student B, "will be thinking of a need of mine that may or may not become apparent. By doing what you are doing, you are not just observing an arbitrary rule. Your act has an ethical component, since it requires attention and consideration. If the essential feature of the creep is self-centered obliviousness, you are the opposite of a creep."

At this point somebody points out that keeping saltshaker and pepper mill together makes it easier to locate them. The next person who needs them will not have to chase them around the table. "By following the rule, then," I conclude, "we show consideration for people we don't even know." The students are intrigued by this unveiling of implications. They talk about the salt and the pepper with their friends and their dates. And they begin to understand that a humble book of etiquette can be used as a primer in moral philosophy. This meditation on good manners and their ethical underpinnings both expands and gives focus to the students' awareness of the needs of others. My hope is that repeated exercises like this will make them less likely to engage in recklessly self-centered—or even abusive—behavior.

2. Acknowledge Others

Acknowledge others' existence, their importance to you, their
feelings, and the things they do for you. Acknowledgment comes
in many forms: remembering someone's name, paying a thoughtful
compliment, summarizing what was just said for a newcomer to
the conversation, holding a door open to let someone through,
welcoming, thanking, and just plain saying hello.

New to the United States, a green graduate student from Italy
eager to understand the world around me, some twenty-five years
ago I rode the bus daily to the UCLA campus in Westwood, California. One of my first powerful impressions of America came
from those rides. Much to my surprise, many passengers would
say, "Good morning," to the driver as they stepped onto the bus
and "Thank you" and "Have a good day" as they stepped off. I
had never witnessed anything like that. In Europe nobody paid
much attention to bus drivers. When I lived in Milan, they had
been for me nearly indistinguishable from the machines they

drove—almost like another anonymous, mechanical part. But on those blue buses of the Santa Monica–Westwood line, thanks to my fellow passengers' acknowledgments, I started to see—to *really* see—the drivers as persons. The ability to look past the job at the individual was an American skill I would continue to learn in the next several years.

A simple "Hello" or "Good morning" is the most basic form of acknowledgment. Every day, when we arrive at our workplaces, we greet our coworkers. As a rule, we don't infuse our greeting with particular intensity. There is no need to. By saying, "Good morning," to Sharon and Rebecca, the secretaries in my department at the university, I automatically acknowledge their existence. Without voicing the thought, I am telling them: *You exist, and this matters to me.* I am also saying: *I know that you monitor—as I do—our relationship; rest assured that, as far as I am concerned, you and I are in reciprocal good standing.* Whenever we are with others, we rely on a system of obligations and expectations. If one morning I failed to say, "Good morning," my omission would beg an explanation. Sharon and Rebecca might wonder whether something they did caused the unexpected change. My greeting may be more cheerful one day and less another, but it always performs its crucial job.

A greeting is a minimal yet meaningful conferral of honor on a person for just being a person. With it, not only do we acknowledge and validate, but we also put at ease and wish well. We announce that we intend no harm and express our concern for the well-being of others. As we do so, we invite others to look upon us with the same benign disposition we have toward them. This is the stuff civility is made of.

And yet we often play the game of invisibility. We see someone we know coming our way, but instead of saying hello or even just nodding our acknowledgment, we proceed as if that someone were invisible or we weren't there. Is a glimmer of acknowledgment in a fleeting encounter so burdensome? Are we shy? Are we lazy? Are we prey to misguided pride? Are we so goal-directed that we won't bother with anything that doesn't advance our progress toward our goal, whatever that might be? Are our souls shrinking beyond repair?

We can't feel gregarious every moment of our lives. At times we will be turned inward, unavailable to others, protective of our space and frame of mind. And that's all right. Sometimes we need that to recharge after the great expenditures of physical and nervous energy required by today's life. We can, however, do without the invisibility game. It is insincere and petty. Let's at least nod each other into existence. And let's not play another game, either, that of waiting to be acknowledged before acknowledging in turn. I hope that we will always have enough self-esteem to feel that being first in greeting doesn't entail loss of face.

THE THREE STRIKES OF INCIVILITY

As Judy waits in line at the bookstore's cash register, a woman nonchalantly slips ahead of her. Where is the harm of that? The rude act—a lack of acknowledgment—causes harm in at least three ways. First of all, Judy is inconvenienced by being made to wait longer. She has other things to do, she needs to complete her business as soon as possible, and she can't.

Second, Judy is harmed by the woman's dismissal of her presence. The woman acts as though Judy didn't exist or her existence didn't matter. The loss of face makes Judy perturbed and resentful.

Third, if Judy feels that she should do something to redress the slight, this will perturb her as well. She will wonder whether she really wants to bring the issue to the woman's attention. Is it worth her while? Will an unpleasant exchange ensue? Is the incident going to escalate? If she doesn't react, is she being cowardly? Yes, rudeness begets conflict with others but also conflict within ourselves, and the latter can prove as hurtful as the former.

3. Think the Best

WE MUST BE AS COURTEOUS TO A MAN AS WE ARE TO A PICTURE,
WHICH WE ARE WILLING TO GIVE THE ADVANTAGE OF A GOOD
LIGHT.   —*Ralph Waldo Emerson*

BE NOT FORGETFUL TO ENTERTAIN STRANGERS: FOR THEREBY
SOME HAVE ENTERTAINED ANGELS UNAWARES.
                                          —*Paul of Tarsus*

I have always found the passage on strangers and angels in the
letter of the Apostle Paul to the Hebrews rich in both meaning
and poetic resonance. The overt meaning is clear: the Apostle is
encouraging the faithful to be generous because there might be
divine messengers among those they will benefit. Whenever I
think of Paul's entrancing words, however, I see a related meaning
developing from them, like a branch growing from a tree trunk.
This second message is: Be generous because, whether you are
aware of it or not, there is a spark of divinity in all of those you
will benefit. Be generous to the angel in all of us. In other words:
think the best of your fellow humans and act accordingly.

Thinking the best of others is a decent thing to do and a way
of keeping a source of healthful innocence in our lives. When we
approach others assuming that they are good, honest, and sensitive,
we often encourage them to be just that. In my role as a teacher,
my drive and enthusiasm in the classroom owe much to my as-

sumption that all of my students are essentially good human beings, interested in the pursuit of knowledge, and willing to work hard. Believing that they are good, I want to be good for them. I feel challenged to match their excellence. Am I deluding myself in thinking the best of them? At times, perhaps I am. But what really counts is that almost all of them will rise to the occasion, riding the tide of my trust. As I think the best of them, they will be shaped by the credit I am willing to give them. They will begin to become what I think they are. This is one of teachers' greatest rewards.

Even outside the classroom I expect that everyone I meet will turn out to be good rather than bad. I have felt this way all of my life. What I find exciting in a new acquaintance is the thought: *Maybe I'm making a discovery here; maybe someone is entering my life who is nice.* That's what gives me joy: the possibility of goodness. I appreciate exceptional intelligence, I can be charmed by beauty, and I am intrigued by charisma. But I will be moved by goodness. Of course I am aware that not all those I meet can be paragons of goodness. Still, my bet with myself is that they will be nice *to me.* I think of my goodwill as an unspoken challenge to them and envision that our lives will be made better by our interaction.

Are you comfortable with who you are and what you have accomplished? Sometimes it is dissatisfaction with ourselves that makes us judge others unfairly. Make sure that you are not projecting onto others the least attractive traits you perceive in yourself. Are you comfortable with change? You may find it difficult to think the best of others if you are made uneasy by a new development—at work, for instance. Whether you like it or not, here you are with a new boss or a new office partner. Do you feel threatened? Does this color your perception of the person involved? Are you making him or her threatening in your mind for no objective reason at all? Are you falling prey to a self-fulfilling prophecy? Try to evaluate the person apart from the situation. Give him or her a fair chance. As a result, you will give the situation a chance to work.

There is no doubt that thinking the best of others can boost the quality of your life. Among other things, it will help you establish rapport with many people who otherwise would remain strangers. Be careful, however, not to overdo it. Thinking the best of others can make us dangerously vulnerable. Your optimism should not be unthinking but rather tempered by the right dose of realism. Having a positive attitude doesn't mean that you should trust just anybody with your life. I do wish that I had been more cautious at various times in my life. And yet thinking the best of my fellow human beings remains a very important part of who I am.

So, when it comes to people, have great expectations: it will be good for your soul, and it may touch theirs. At the same time, don't discount the possibility of unpleasant surprises. If people let you down, don't rush to judgment, but don't disregard the disenchanting evidence, either. Sad as it may be, accept that your opinion and feelings are changing. At some point, you may decide to tell the people who have disappointed you about your discontent. Be frank. No matter what their reaction to your frankness may be, you can at least take comfort in thinking that you will have given them a precious chance to learn something about themselves, you, or both.

A NOTE ON THE FAIR AMERICANS

People from other parts of the world are often struck by Americans' seemingly unbounded willingness to take a chance on others. This is a defining American trait, just like the belief in freedom and in the rights of the individual. What is America if not the place where people can expect to be given a chance, where they are given the benefit of the doubt when they come under suspicion and a second chance after a fall? These are all forms of thinking the best of others. As a European who has lived in the United States for a long time, I continue to marvel at this mixture of idealism and radical fairness in the American soul.

4. Listen

Vivian Gussin Paley tells the story of Dominick and Abby, two
fifth-graders visiting an art museum with their classmates. The
docent brings an artifact to the children's attention. It is a lighted
multicolored neon tube.

"What do you think the artist had in mind?" she asks the
children. At first no one answers, but then a boy offers a
statement of fact. "This can't go in a house that don't have
lights, you know." Before the docent can respond, the teacher
bends over and whispers, "Stop being silly, Dominick!" A
few children giggle.

But not the girl next to him. While several of the other
students attempt an answer to the docent's question, Abby

speaks quietly to Dominick. "Do you mean, like if someone is poor and didn't pay the electric bill? So then that thing wouldn't work?"

Dominick nods gratefully. "Yeah. Or you could live on the top of a mountain," he says, "and there ain't even any wires going up there. So they can just have a *picture* of it, see, not this kind of thing." The teacher frowns at them and the two children stop talking. But they sit up straighter and each carries the look of a secret sharer.

Paley sees Abby's remark as prompted by an impulse to rescue Dominick from embarrassment. Her point is that children can be genuinely kind, and that they are endowed with the instinct to help those in distress. She wonders whether the two children have a sense of the importance of what they have done together. "They have created," she concludes, "a moment of mutual respect and dignity that seems, in itself, a work of art."

Abby shows the skills of the good listener. Having paid attention—real attention—to her friend's observation, she makes sure she understood it correctly. She asks him a question that allows him to clarify what he has in mind. This is a smart, kind, and civil strategy of listening, one that not many adults either master or are willing to use. When we manage to do what Abby does, we show those around us that we are interested in their words and therefore in their feelings. We let them know that we value not only the message but also the messenger. This is listening at its best.

What prevents us from doing a good job of listening is that instead of focusing on other people, we focus on ourselves and our own needs. This is what we do, for instance, when we interrupt. We just can't sit still—and silent—as someone else speaks, for we feel the urge to seize the limelight for ourselves. Thus we will rudely push others offstage. Along with narcissism, a power game is sometimes involved here. Taking control of the conversational flow makes us feel as though we have control over our partners in speech.

Sudden redirections of attention are interruptions as well. Although your interlocutor has completed his or her sentence, this gives you no license to leave it unacknowledged as you rush to utter one of your own. Unfortunately, "disregard and proceed" is one of the most common patterns in verbal exchanges, even among friends. I suspect that some of my friends may have found me at fault when it comes to this conversational sin. A colleague tells me over the telephone that she went to Florida for a vacation. Instead of asking *her* how *her* vacation was, I hasten to tell her how *I* feel about Florida. I quickly add what *I* like to do when *I* am there. And finally, I break the fascinating news that I was there two years ago, didn't go last winter, but hope to return the next. The result: my colleague's experience and feelings get lost completely in my inane and self-centered rambling.

This disregard-and-proceed pattern is very common in the workplace, especially among competitive people. Over lunch at their company's cafeteria, an excited and proud Pedro tells David how he, Pedro, has been able to eliminate a snag in the marketing strategy for the new software their company is promoting. Barely letting Pedro complete his account of the events, David redirects the conversation toward his own most recent exploit in programming wizardry. A mild resentment on Pedro's part ensues. A major offense? Perhaps not. A clear case of insensitive behavior, which— if followed by other similar breaches of good manners—could eventually mar the relationship between the two coworkers? No doubt about it.

We are ineffective listeners when we let our past experiences interfere with the attention we should give to our present moments. For instance, we often let what we already know—or believe we know—of others alter our perception of what they are telling us at this very moment, in this unique set of circumstances. "Knowing" Tea, we "know" what she is going to say on budget allocations before she opens her mouth—little incentive to listen there. And we may tune Jason out because we "know" that he has never contributed anything of substance to our neighborhood renovation committee. In either case, we are not prepared to do justice to what Tea or Jason may contribute *now*.

Oftentimes it is not the past but the future that makes us poor listeners. When we listen with the future in mind, we are focused not on the speaker but rather on the outcome of our verbal exchange. We let the pursuit of our own goals take precedence over everything else. If you were telling me about a painful experience of yours, you would trust implicitly that my first concern wouldn't be how to use that information to my advantage. You would expect and be grateful for my disinterested attention.

Now, I am not suggesting that we should completely ignore past experience and abstain from pursuing personal goals when we interact with others. That would be not only impossible but also unwise. I am saying that as listeners we have an obligation to concentrate on just listening *before* doing anything else.

Good listening has three basic components. When you are ready to listen: (1) plan your listening; (2) show that you are listening; (3) be a cooperative listener.

- **Plan your listening.** Listen with no other intention than that of listening. Make the conscious effort of making listening your goal. Say to yourself: *I'm going to* listen *now; this is the time to* just *listen; I am going to* make time *to listen.* Silence is, of course, your tool of choice. Being able to listen is, before anything else, being able to remain silent so that someone else can speak. Rediscover the power and allure of silence—your silence and that of the world around you. Since you want to give the other person your undivided attention, eliminate sources of distraction. Turn off your television set and your cellular telephone. Finally, put out of your mind your next errands and appointments. Remember, your goal is to stay focused on the present.

- **Show that you are listening.** You want the other person to know that you are taking the task of listening seriously. Establish eye contact. Give the occasional nod. Interject brief expressions that show that your thoughts are not wandering and encourage the speaker to continue: "Yes," "Right," "I understand," "I didn't know that," "I see." Once in a while you may want to reconfigure in your own words your interlocutor's message to verify that you understood the point he or she is trying to make. "I just don't know what to do," Mia tells her friend Teresa, "I've tried all my daughter's life to encourage her and to let her make her own decisions. I thought that would boost her self-esteem. And I thought she was well adjusted. But now she seems defiant and out of control. She snaps at me all the time, telling me it's her life and she knows what's good for her. Maybe I should have been more of a disciplinarian. All I know is that I'm really worried." This is the time for Teresa to restate briefly what she has heard: "Alice being rebellious makes you second-guess yourself as a parent. Now, do you really think that the problem is that you may have not given her enough structure and discipline?"

- **Be a cooperative listener.** Teresa didn't rush to agree or disagree with her friend. She simply showed that she understood the issues at hand and gently invited Mia to focus. "Can it also be," she continues, "that Alice is just going through a difficult time for reasons you don't know?" As Mia pursues the "it's my fault" line of thinking, she may also decide to find out whether something other than her parenting holds the key to her daughter's rebelliousness. There is a point where listening becomes a fully collaborative enterprise. Cooperative listening means separating what is important from what is not. It means helping give shape and direction to what the other person says while also trying to understand what he or she is trying to say, not only with words but with body language as well. Cooperative listening has to do with asking the right questions (open-ended questions in particular, of the "How do you feel about that?," "What are the alternatives?," and "What do you think would help?" variety). And it has to do with stopping short of intruding. Rather than satisfying your curiosity, helping the speaker achieve a higher level of clarity should be the goal of your questions.

Finally, although you may be forming your opinions on what is being said, voice them only if you have a clear sense that that is what your interlocutor expects you to do and if you are comfortable with doing so. The same rule applies to giving advice.

Not every verbal exchange requires the same level of listening concentration. Good listening is hard work. Since our supply of energy is limited, investing it judiciously is part of wisdom. Let's never forget that the quality of our listening is as good a measure of our humanity as any.

Human beings want someone to listen to them. In the midst of a culture that glorifies indulgent self-expression, we may find it difficult to attend patiently to the words of others. It may not occur to us that when we find the strength to engage in considerate listening we are in fact expressing ourselves. At our best.

5. Be Inclusive

IT TAKES A VARIETY OF PEOPLE TO CHALLENGE US, ENCOURAGE US, PROMOTE US, AND MOST OF ALL, HELP US ACHIEVE A BROADER DIMENSION OF OURSELVES.   —*Glenn Van Ekeren*

"THE GREAT SECRET, ELIZA, IS NOT HAVING BAD MANNERS OR GOOD MANNERS OR ANY OTHER PARTICULAR SORT OF MANNERS, BUT HAVING THE SAME MANNER FOR ALL HUMAN SOULS: IN SHORT, BEHAVING AS IF YOU WERE IN HEAVEN, WHERE THERE ARE NO THIRD-CLASS CARRIAGES, AND ONE SOUL IS AS GOOD AS ANOTHER."   —*George Bernard Shaw*

While on a trip to Italy, Carol was having a pleasant and lively meal with her new Italian acquaintances. It was a tightknit group, but much to her delight, they had invited her to spend yet another evening with them and she felt she was getting close to them. They were all speaking Italian since Carol, a native speaker of English, understood and spoke the local language well. Only once in a while would she miss a beat.

Mauro said something very funny very fast. All the Italian friends laughed at the joke, and Carol laughed along with them. Even before her laughter subsided, however, Mauro turned to her and said sharply in English: "Why are you laughing if you haven't understood a word?" Her laughter fading to a thin smile, she looked at him as if she were going to say something. Perhaps having made a split-second decision not to upset the good cheer of the table, she turned instead toward another friend, as if nothing had happened. After that, however, some friends noticed that Carol seemed subdued. For her, the evening had lost its shine.

A lapse in civility can be anything but trivial when we look at it from the receiving end. It's easy to mindlessly spoil someone's happy moment. Whether or not Carol understood Mauro's joke is irrelevant. Maybe her laughter had little to do with his joke and simply expressed her happiness at being with her newfound friends. Maybe she didn't want to be left out. She *needed* to laugh along with everybody else. Mauro should have respected that need rather than questioning her sincerity (and linguistic competence). Now, his challenge might have been only half-serious—an invitation to lighthearted banter. The effect, however, was to confirm Carol in her role of outsider. Whatever he meant, the message she heard was: *You don't belong; you're not welcome; you are not one of us.*

One of our strongest yearnings is to be accepted by others. We love being welcomed by individuals, and we delight in the feeling of belonging to a group. Part of our identity is shaped by and within groups; within our groups we find shelter, meaning, and direction. Thus attitudes and words that exclude rather than include are rarely funny. In most cases they hurt.

Shouldn't we be allowed to draw boundaries as we go through our everyday lives? Of course we should. We owe it to both ourselves and others to become good at defining and protecting our own spaces. But we should be careful never to engage in self-serving, unfair, and mean-spirited strategies of exclusion. Being inclusive means applying the principle of respect for persons to all persons. When it comes time to show respect and consideration to others, we do not pick and choose.

Selective conferral of respect is a commonly used weapon in the power games played by men and women of all ages.

When I ask high schoolers to give me examples of uncivil behavior, snubbing is always among the first serious infractions they mention. They tell me of their peers who selectively ignore others in conversation or who get up from a cafeteria table when someone they don't like joins them. And then there is that ever-recurring heartbreak: not being popular or glamorous or wealthy enough to be invited to the gilded get-togethers of the charmed elite.

The workplace, where power, rank, and money are at stake, is a breeding ground for cliques as well. Although allegiance to a division, a team, or a group can be productive, a clique mentality is in the long run detrimental to both workers and organizations. Identifying with our group can be good as long as we are willing to work with others outside. There always comes a time to switch from the competitive to the cooperative mode.

There are many ways to be inclusive in the workplace, from trying to work effectively with a person we don't like to accepting graciously a new coworker in our midst. When someone joins our workplace, how many of us make a conscious effort to make him or her feel welcome?

No workplace in the world is as diverse as the American one. Fostering a workplace culture of civil openness and inclusion is clearly in the interest of most American organizations today. This is the culture of the future, which will allow organizations to do well in the global civilization of the new millennium. Let's make an effort to get closer to those who are different from us and with whom we usually don't associate. Let's give them a chance by approaching them as free of prejudice as possible, with genuine respect and a kind disposition.

As we advance in years, we often seek safety in sameness. Rather than yearning to discover, we want to be reassured. It is almost a duty toward ourselves and others, however, to resist, at least occasionally, the temptation of the well-rehearsed life. Making the effort to diversify our acquaintances and experiences and to understand that which we discover is certainly a civil thing to do. It happens to be a smart one as well.

THE INCLUSIVE MIND-SET: A LIST OF SUGGESTIONS

- Reevaluate your dislikes. Are they all warranted? Are you at ease with all of them? Are you fettered by habit and inertia? Is change long overdue?

- Try speaking and listening to somebody you never liked.

- Make the effort of spending a few minutes with somebody you always found uninteresting.

- When you have several listeners, do not turn to just one or two of them while treating others as though they weren't there.

- At a social gathering, choose conversation topics that can be enjoyed by all present. Make sure that no one feels excluded. If you happen to know an interest of someone who seems shy or intimidated, steer the conversation in that direction.

- Summarize the contents of an ongoing conversation for a newcomer.

- If you are responsible for teamwork, elicit input from all team members.

- If you are making plans with a coworker for an impromptu cafeteria lunch, include any other coworker who is present at that moment.

- If you know more than one language, speak the one known by all or most of those present. Don't use your linguistic knowledge to communicate with some while shutting out others. This, of course, applies to both the social and professional sides of your life.

- Make a new neighbor feel welcome by just stopping by to say, "Welcome."

- Tell a new in-law, "Welcome to the family."

- Welcome a new colleague who has just moved to your town. Set aside time to help him or her understand and adjust to the new work environment. Give him or her tips about life in town.

- Develop and show an interest in cultures other than your own. This does not require that you endorse enthusiastically every aspect of every one of them. It is civil of you to consider different mores and values with an open mind. Nobody, however, should expect or demand that you adopt these mores and values as your own.

6. Speak Kindly

Speaking with consideration and kindness is at the heart of civil behavior. To speak kindly you need to be aware constantly that you are speaking to living, breathing, vulnerable human beings. Don't discount the power of your words. The thought that they might cause unnecessary hurt or discomfort should inform every conversation. When you speak kindly to others, you manage to keep *them* in mind as you speak—which means keeping at bay, at least for a while, the pressing demands of *your* needs. By speaking with kindness you will improve the lives of those around you. Your words of kindness can inspire others, rescue them from despair, and reconcile them with life. Or, at the very least, you will lift their spirits and make their day more endurable.

Make sure that you need to speak. (Sometimes silence can be kinder and more considerate than words.) When you speak you want to make a genuine contribution to the verbal exchange of which you are part. Are you making it go forward? Are you bringing to it a good example from personal experience? Are you adding a new, useful perspective? Are you building upon what was just said? If you are, your words are a definite improvement over silence. You also happen to be kind, since you are not wasting someone's time and you are addressing him or her in a spirit of cooperation.

Take a few seconds to figure out what kind of contribution the circumstances require. Are the two of you simply exchanging information? Is the other person instead expecting words of support or maybe asking for your advice? If you are not certain, ask that person to clarify his or her needs and expectations. You don't want misunderstanding to mar your exchange from the start.

Speak at an unhurried pace so that you are easily understood, try to make your point as clearly as possible, and avoid going off on a tangent. Stop when you have made your point so that others can speak in turn. Solicit their input whenever you think it's appropriate. By choosing your words and building your sentences with care you will do justice to yourself and to those listening to you. Being articulate, however, is not tantamount to being glib, pretentious, or overbearing. Speaking kindly should never turn into a narcissistic performance.

Keep the volume of your voice moderate at all times, no matter where you are, no matter with whom you are speaking. A loud voice can easily annoy; it can also sound intimidating and even threatening. Never yell at anybody. Remember that people always respond to the tone of your voice. Showing kindness is as much a matter of tone as it is one of words. If your anger shows in your tone of voice, explain the reasons for your feelings as rationally and sedately as possible. And yes, you can be angry, show your anger, and be civil at the same time.

Should you need to cope with conflict, do so in a fair fashion: you owe it to yourself as much as to your opponents. Never utter unkind words regarding their identity (racial, national, sexual, or otherwise) and other aspects of their personal life that are essentially irrelevant to the contested issues at hand. Instead of looking for any vulnerable areas to attack in a strategy of overkill, try to address directly the substance of the issues. Throughout the confrontation never lose sight of the humanity of your opponents. Resist the temptation to think of them as faceless, nameless agents of the "wrong side." No matter how much you happen to disagree with their ideas or positions, never cease to feel that they are entitled to at least a modicum of sympathetic understanding. That will help you start working toward a negotiated solution.

Civil conversation has no place for profanities. Many find it unsettling to be exposed to them. Certain profanities do offend—and sometimes painfully so—religious sensibilities. Quite apart from that, a language laced with curses and vulgar expressions can be perceived as distasteful, hostile, and abusive. Although you may not object strongly to this kind of language, you want to be considerate of those who do and refrain from using it even on occasion.

Never embarrass or mortify. Respect for others requires that you don't make them the targets of sarcastic remarks, you don't belittle them or their accomplishments, and you don't laugh at them. All these behaviors are clearly demeaning and/or aggressive. In a more subtle way, so is bragging. Bragging is often merely a ladder we build for ourselves out of words when we are afraid we are not tall enough in the eyes of the world. It is an unwitting confession to low self-esteem. When we brag we emphasize how much better than others we think we are. To put is very simply, bragging is not kind. And by the way, there is no such thing as bragging *rights*.

Always think before speaking. That your words are kind rather than unkind and that they will be perceived as such should be one of your paramount concerns. With your kind words you build a shelter of sanity and trust into which you welcome others for a much-needed respite. If you manage to make this way of speaking part of what you are, the quality of your relationships will substantially increase and with it the overall quality of your everyday life.

ON THE KINDNESS OF BODY LANGUAGE

Smile. Many believe that if they smile they will be taken less seriously and will relinquish control, especially at work. In my opinion, there aren't many drawbacks to a good, sincere, and well-placed smile. With it you show that you have self-confidence, that you are relaxed and open to contact, and that you trust the person in front of you. Don't be afraid to smile, if for no other reason than it is an easy way to brighten somebody's day.

Turning both your face and body toward your interlocutor will show that you are committed to communicating. Convey your interest in what the other person has to say by leaning forward (ever so slightly). Occasional slight nods of your head show that your attention is not lagging and that you understand. Perhaps the best way to show interest and attunement is through sustained eye contact and the adjusting of your facial expressions to reflect what the person is saying. Touching someone's hand or arm as you listen or as you speak may also be appropriate.

The importance of body language was revealed to me a few years ago in a Maryland maximum security prison. One of the inmates came to talk to me at the end of a workshop on civility. He wanted to let me know how much something that had happened a couple of hours earlier had meant to him. "Do you know what you did when I approached you out of the blue to introduce myself?" he asked. I replied that I didn't. "Instead of freezing or stepping back, you leaned closer to talk to me. You didn't know, but I was testing you. You passed the test."

7 . Don't Speak Ill

NOBODY EVER GOSSIPS ABOUT OTHER PEOPLE'S SECRET
VIRTUES.
                              —*Bertrand Russell*

Your new teacher is a very *nice* woman; you'll like her." "We met such a *nice* couple last night!" "People in this office are *nice*; I know you'll feel welcome here." Although our values may be in a phase of dramatic transition, we still utter every day these traditional (and comforting) assessments of character. By and large, the first, the important, the defining thing we want to know about our fellow humans is whether they are nice. In many instances, of course, "nice" itself goes unexplained since we all know—more or less—what it means. Sometimes, however, we feel compelled to single out and recognize an exceptional trait of the "nice" person in question. One such special trait is the ability to go through life without speaking ill of others. "He is a very nice man. I've known him all of my life and *I have never heard him say a mean word about anyone.*" Chances are that you have summarized the core of someone's humanity in such a fashion once or twice. I know I have, and I also know it would give me great pleasure if someone spoke of me in these terms.

What makes us speak ill of others?

- When we are unsure of our own worth we project upon others the less-than-flattering image we have of ourselves.

- Finding in others faults we don't think we have makes us feel good.

- When we are in competition with others, sometimes we can't help believing that we will shine by contrast if we make them look bad.

- It is less demanding and less painful to point out other people's problems—real or imaginary—than to try to solve our own.

- By disparaging those who wronged us we exact our revenge.

- By showing that we are privy to an unflattering secret about someone we seek to raise our standing in our group. At the same time, we may feel empowered because what we say can cause considerable damage.

- By putting down someone who is not present, we seek to establish a complicity of sorts with someone who is. We take comfort, that is, in the assumption that we who are present are good and the absent are bad. This gives us the impression that we are strengthening our connection with those around us.

Today the Internet provides a new forum for verbal attacks. Workplace electronic message boards have been used for quite some time by employees to fire off inappropriate and offensive remarks against coworkers. Internet anonymity is all too often an irresistible temptation for the sulky and the gossipy. Many seem to look at cyberspace as an ethically vacant space, one in which the rules of traditional everyday decency don't apply. But an anonymous letter is an anonymous letter regardless of the medium used to send it. It is as unacceptable in the computer age as it was in that of the partner desk. Use the electronic equipment at work only for job-related tasks and in a responsible and professional manner. And remember that when it comes to the new information technology, anonymity often turns out to be an illusion.

Why shouldn't we speak ill of others?

- When we speak of others in a derogatory manner we hurt them. We always hurt their reputation, and we can also hurt their feelings should our words reach them.

- Our disparaging remarks against X can be taken by some as an authorization to unleash abuse against X.

- It is cowardly to attack those who are not present. They cannot defend themselves and the attacker can get away with misrepresentations, exaggerations, and outright lies.

- Our speaking unkindly of others may be severely judged by those who are listening to us. When we threaten someone else's reputation we put our own at risk as well.

- As we speak ill of others we can make those who are listening to us uncomfortable or even angry. One doesn't have to be the target of unkind words to be offended and hurt by them.

- Our disparaging words against X can prompt X to retaliate, and not only verbally. The possibility of things spiraling out of control is always present. We know for a fact that many acts of violence have their origin in acts of incivility.

What are we to do when someone speaks ill of others in our presence? Depending on the situation, we can:

- Leave.

- Remain silent (especially if the disparaging is short-lived and mild in nature).

- Say something positive about the absent victim and/or change the subject.

- Openly communicate to the attacker that we are ill at ease and unwilling to play the game: "You know, I am really not comfortable discussing this"; "I would prefer not to speculate about the details of his personal life"; "It doesn't seem fair to make these allegations in her absence, does it?"

I find disparaging talk difficult to bear. In fact, rather than really listening to the bad things Y has to say about X, I often drift off thinking about Y and me. I could as easily be the subject of his malicious speech. My luck is that I'm present and X's misfortune is that he is not. Tomorrow, however, the roles could be reversed, with me cast as the victim.

Doesn't Y realize that I may think less of him because of what he's saying? Doesn't he care if he tarnishes his own image? Then it occurs to me that when it comes to speaking ill of others I am not without fault. Although I do care about what others think of me, I still haven't managed to completely eliminate unkind remarks from my conversational repertoire. I can only take some comfort in having made it a priority of mine to try.

I urge you to try as well. When people get used to hearing you speaking only neutrally or kindly of others they will not be afraid to open up and get close to you because they know you will not betray them. Thus you will be rewarded with meaningful relationships that otherwise would never have come into being.

ON MAKING NICE

Perhaps because I am not a native speaker of English, I am intrigued by the expression "make nice." I know that it is addressed to children who have been squabbling. I know that it simply means "make up; settle down and be friends; make peace." But the *make* in "make nice" always makes me think. "Nice" is something that must be built, something that doesn't simply happen or come to us out of the blue but instead requires work. Good social interaction demands a deliberate effort, an act of will. Part of the gratification that we derive from the exercise of civility has to do with the investment of energy involved. "Nice" is something we *make*. In whatever form it manifests itself, it is always a small triumph over stolid and stalling pride, moral torpor, and plain, dulling inertia.

8. Accept and Give Praise

THE DEEPEST PRINCIPLE IN HUMAN NATURE IS THE CRAVING
TO BE APPRECIATED.   —*William James*

I CAN LIVE FOR TWO MONTHS ON A GOOD COMPLIMENT.
                                                      —*Mark Twain*

In the Middle Ages the bestowing of praise was looked upon as a characteristic of the magnanimous—the noble at heart. It was obvious then, just as it is now, that praise we give to others flows, at least in part, from a transcending of our Selves. The inclination to express sincere praise (as opposed to flattery) continues to be a most captivating character trait of the civil.

As children we all love to be praised by our parents, the most important persons in our lives. We are thrilled by their attention and bask in the sun of validation that comes with their approval. We take our parents' praise as both a manifestation of their love for us and proof that we are worthy of that love—a heady mixture indeed. Born and reinforced during the very first, formative years of our lives, our taste for being praised never goes away.

Praising others, however, does not always come easily. One main reason is that when we give praise we may feel as though we are relinquishing control. The more we manage to bring ourselves to give praise, however, the less vulnerable we feel. After a while, as we make others feel good about themselves by praising them, we feel good about ourselves as well.

Here are a few good reasons to engage in the generous form of attention that is praise.

- By sharing with others how we feel about them, we let them know something about ourselves and strengthen the bonds between us in the process.

- By saying, "What you are doing is wonderful," we encourage those who are doing the wonderful thing to keep doing it. Maybe in a small way, we become responsible for the continued existence of something wonderful.

- Many are unaware of their own gifts or may not realize how outstanding those gifts are. Through our praise we reveal to people who they are.

- Giving praise we nurture others' self-esteem, a crucial factor in their emotional well-being.

Experts on manners across the centuries have provided instruction on how to handle praise. They actually prefer to speak of "compliments," a category in which they include all kinds of praise, from the serious to the mundane. A compliment, they tell us, is a gift, one we are expected to acknowledge with the simple courtesy of a firm and felt "Thank you." All too often, instead, we add self-deprecating remarks ("Oh, I'm not sure I was *that* good"). That reaction to praise is almost like returning a gift we didn't like. At the opposite end of the spectrum, we should never solicit more praise than we were given or expand on a compliment we received ("I *was* good, wasn't I, and you know what? I am getting better every day!"). Of course, should we receive by mistake compliments that belong to others, we will give credit where it is due.

OTHER DOS AND DON'TS OF COMPLIMENTS

- Don't pay a compliment unless it is sincere.

- Don't refrain from paying a compliment thinking that your feelings are already known.

- Don't confuse complimenting with patronizing.

- Don't hasten to reciprocate a compliment. If you do, you give the impression that the compliment you received was difficult for you to handle and you felt compelled to rid yourself of it at the first opportunity.

- Word your compliments carefully. Those who receive them will thus know that you have given serious thought to what they did and feel even more validated. Whenever appropriate, make the effort to be specific. "Good job on your presentation!" is a good, serviceable compliment. But sometimes you may want to say: "I'm impressed. I hadn't heard someone argue his points so clearly, logically, and forcefully in a long time. I particularly admired . . ."

- Start with a person in mind. You needn't always wait for *something* to strike you as worthy of a compliment. Focus on *someone* and ask yourself: what is it that this person does that deserves recognition?

- Rarely do we have the opportunity to compliment someone on something of great import. Why not look for something small, then? You can make someone's day by admiring his or her taste in wine, wallpaper, shoes, or cars.

- Glenn Van Ekeren has a list of simple phrases that can help us express our feelings of praise and appreciation. Here is a selection: "I appreciate the way you . . ."; "Thanks for going all out when you . . ."; "One of the things I enjoy most about you is . . ."; "Our team couldn't be successful without your . . ."; "You did an outstanding job of . . ."; "It's evident you have the ability to . . ."; I admire the way you take the time to . . ."; "What a great idea!"; "You're doing a top-notch job of . . ."

COMPLIMENTS IN THE WORKPLACE

Compliments on a job well done are part of a healthy workplace culture. Surveys of opinion have shown over and over again that employees rank appreciation and recognition at the top of their lists of motivating factors in the workplace. Thus it is not surprising to find in U.S. Labor Department statistics that feeling unappreciated at work is a leading cause of leaving a job. It is a widely shared opinion that the willingness to praise and reward is an essential asset for leaders at any level of any organization. Many managers in the contemporary workplace are tough but emotionally alive coaches ready to make their players feel good about themselves by praising them not only for superb performances but also for trying hard.

A sincere and straightforward work-related compliment is always appropriate and welcome in any workplace. Compliments that are not work-related, however, are often problematic. A consensus has been emerging that compliments on attire and physical appearance do not belong in the workplace at all. Whether your coworker strikes you as attractively dressed or just plain attractive, keep your impressions to yourself. It is the professional thing to do—among other things, it keeps misunderstandings at bay. Nonverbal communication should, of course, follow suit. Leering is unacceptable and so is any other kind of suggestive demeanor. Remember that in today's workplace the uncivil, offensive, flirtatious foolishness of yesteryear is rarely tolerated. You don't want to discover how sadly ineffectual the I-didn't-mean-anything-by-it defense can be.

9. Respect Even a Subtle "No"

ACCEPTANCE IS THE TRUEST KINSHIP WITH HUMANITY.
                                    —*Gilbert Keith Chesterton*

Someone has turned down your request or invitation and you won't take no for an answer. Bad idea and bad form—to say the least. Respecting the "No" of another is one of the most elementary and significant rules of respect. Refrain from interrogating. When someone declines your invitation, asking why is both intrusive and guilt-inducing. Instead, you might say, "I just want you to know that we'd be glad to have you. If not this, maybe another time."

Your coworker has shown little interest in contributing to an office collection: don't pester her. Your vegetarian dinner companion has already refused the meat loaf: don't insist that he "just taste it." It's late and your date has chosen not to go dancing after all: your obstinate urging is not charming. You can be cordial, spirited, and even enthusiastic without making a nuisance of yourself.

Respecting "No" is of the essence in the romantic arena. Be realistic in your expectations. There *is* the possibility that the person who has caught your eye won't be interested in you. Be ready to accept that. The two of you may get closer and even intimate, or you may not. What is certain is that you want to be remembered as someone who never faltered in respecting the other person's right to decide for him- or herself.

Learn to recognize a "No" when it's not stated in the most explicit of ways. If the stranger sitting beside you on the plane is paying more attention to his or her laptop computer screen than to your attempts at starting a conversation, that's a "No" and you must respect it. If your in-laws appear less than enthusiastic at the news that you are planning to leave your children with them for the weekend, don't ignore their clues. They are tactfully expressing their "No." Realize that you may have been taking them for granted, apologize, and make other plans. One of the fundamental principles of decent behavior is to care enough for others not to make our problems theirs.

We frequently fail to understand or choose to ignore signs of reluctance in others. When that happens, we end up making others do what they would rather not or we force them to flat out say, "No," upsetting them in the process. This is not civil.

Why is it difficult to take "No" for an answer? Because the child in us, the two-year-old who stubbornly wants to have things his or her way, never completely disappears. In many cases, this is compounded by a self-esteem problem. We often take a "No" as a rejection of our whole being. Therefore, we equate that "No" with a serious threat to our self-image. Thus the more we are able to say, "Yes," to ourselves, the better we will be at graciously accepting a "No" from others. The way we treat others always depends on the health of our sense of Self.

GOOD MANNERS AGAINST ABUSE

Do you think it's better for people to have good manners, even if it means hiding what they really think, or is it better for them to express what they really think, even if it's bad manners to do so? The question is not mine. It is part of a questionnaire that ABC News distributed a couple of years ago to find out how Americans felt about good manners in general and about the state of American manners in particular. About 56 percent of the respondents said that it is better for people to have good manners, while 38 percent responded that it is better for them to express what they really think.

The numbers are interesting and rather encouraging, but the formulation of the question itself is equally interesting, since it connects good manners to something bad (the hiding of one's real thoughts) and bad manners to something good (the expressing of one's real thoughts). This is a common way of framing the philosophy of manners, and, indeed, it's not totally unwarranted. I wonder, however, how respondents would answer if good manners were connected to restraint and self-control, rather than to concealment, and bad manners to intemperance and abuse, rather than to sincerity. Undoubtedly the numbers would be even more encouraging.

We need more good manners in order to improve the quality of our lives. But we will have more good manners in our lives only when we are able to develop a new language to speak about them. And it has to be a new language that makes them relevant for both the older and the new generations. A training in good manners is a training in sensitivity. Thus good manners are a precious resource in the fight against a number of ills afflicting us today, including violence. It is along these lines that we can promote a rediscovery of a wealth of wisdom that our society clearly needs.

10. Respect Others' Opinions

IF ALL MANKIND MINUS ONE WERE OF ONE OPINION, AND ONLY ONE PERSON WERE OF CONTRARY OPINION, MANKIND WOULD BE NO MORE JUSTIFIED IN SILENCING THAT ONE PERSON THAN HE, IF HE HAD THE POWER, WOULD BE JUSTIFIED IN SILENCING MANKIND.
                                        —*John Stuart Mill*

Respecting others' opinions is part of a larger attitude of respect—respect for the whole person—that we are expected to develop as we grow up. Respect for opinions is not an easy art at all. It requires self-esteem, self-control, sensitivity, tolerance, fairness, and generosity. And it applies both to stated opinions and to opinions that are left unspoken.

There are at least two ways of showing disrespect for others on account of what they think. One is by telling them that their opinions are crazy, stupid, worthless, and the like. The other is by assuming that what we think must be what they think also. Respecting others' opinions doesn't mean being untrue to our own. It simply requires us to recognize that others are entitled to look at the world differently and that when they share their views with us they can expect a fair hearing.

Since what we believe is an integral part of who we are, we tend to perceive criticism directed at our opinions as rejection. When that happens, defensiveness and resentment can put an end to dialogue. This means that we should follow good protocols of disagreement. If possible and appropriate:

- Save the core of someone else's opinion even as you qualify your acceptance: "Yes, I agree that what you say may be true in general, but there are circumstances when . . ."

- Recognize that although you don't agree, what you hear is not unreasonable: "Indeed, that idea can be appealing; however . . ."

- Allow that if you knew more, your opinion might change: "I don't know, it doesn't seem right, but perhaps there is more here than meets the eye."

- Make generous use of the metaphor of perspective: "Yes, but if you look at it from a different point of view . . ."

All these are forms of qualified disagreement, which in most circumstances are preferable to absolute disagreement. Through them you will usually manage to take the sting off your challenge. If, however, the opinion in question is repugnant to you, feel free to reject it outright: "I'm sorry, I believe this is wrong"; "I disagree, I find this opinion offensive"; "You know, this really goes against my principles."

The way we react when we don't agree depends on where we are, with whom, and what we are doing. Someone argues that more public funding should go to private schools, an opinion you don't share. At a PTA or a town meeting, you can take your time to present a detailed, forceful argument against it. As an invited guest at a dinner table, however, you may decide to ignore the issue. Or you may briefly state why you disagree before turning to a less controversial subject. In other words, you may want to balance your desire to state your convictions with your concern for the convivial fellowship that your host has worked so hard at fostering. In general, a meal, any meal, is not the best venue for a political debate.

Many speak as though their opinions were necessarily shared by everybody around them. This presumptive sharing can originate in simple lack of sensitivity or it can be a deliberate, if covert, way of saying: "If you don't think like me you should. Start now!" Either way, it is bullying. You support political candidate X and his plan for industrial pollution control, which is opposed by candidate Y. Resist the temptation to declare to your coworkers in the cafeteria: "It's going to be X by a landslide. Voters can't be so dumb that they won't see through Y's shenanigans." Of course, somebody at the table may very well be a supporter of candidate Y's policies. You are entitled to your political preferences, but others are also entitled to hear them expressed in a civil way.

We are all victims, at one time or another, of presumptive opinion sharing. I find myself drawn over and over again into playing the worn-out game of television bashing. There is always someone who thinks it's time to remind me that television is awful and harmful to me and the rest of humanity. This is presented as a self-evident truth upon which everybody with a semblance of a brain agrees and which should, therefore, go unexamined. I am thus expected to join in the jeremiad with a disconsolate shaking of my head.

Whenever I am exposed to the lamentations and fulminations of the television-is-trash cohorts, I'm inevitably ill at ease. Strange as it may seem, I believe that there are good programs on television. The thousands of men and women who work in that business deserve better than a blanket indictment as producers of junk. But all this is almost beside the point. The point is that I resent finding myself inducted into a club I didn't ask to join. Those who operate according to the I'm-sure-you're-one-of-us assumption think on our behalf. They dismiss the notion that we might have a different opinion. This is, for lack of a better word, rude.

Those with views different from yours may refrain from revealing them to preserve the harmony of the conversation. Or they may choose not to challenge you because they feel intimidated by you. Aware that they are giving the impression they agree with an opinion when in fact they don't, they may feel frustrated. Spare them. Present your opinions as just *opinions*, rather than transcendental truths. Make room for disagreement. Invite feedback. Among the most civil utterances of all time is the simple, humble, and smart question, "What do *you* think?" Let's use it generously. Who knows, we may learn something by listening in earnest to an opposing view. We may even discover that our opinion is not as good as we thought it was and that it is time for us to change, time to expand our horizons.

11. Mind Your Body

THE IDEA IS TO ATTRACT, NOT REPEL.   *—Peggy and Peter Post*

When looking closely at civility, I marvel at how many ways there are of showing respect to ourselves and those around us. Minding our bodies is one of them, and certainly not a minor consideration. We all know that we can offend others with our bodies. We do that with the way our bodies look, the way they smell, and what we do with and to them. Thus we all need to become conversant with the civility of body management, which begins with good basic grooming habits. When we take good care of our bodies and our appearance we implicitly validate who we are. We look at ourselves as deserving of attention and act upon that feeling. As we are being good to ourselves, we also show that we consider others important. Behind the attention to our grooming are the goals of appearing at our best on the stage of everyday life and of being as pleasant a presence for others as we can.

Essential to good grooming are a clean and odor-free body, recently washed hair, finger- and toenails in perfect order, a close shave, well-applied makeup, if worn, and clean teeth and fresh breath. Also essential are clean and unrumpled clothes, well-kept shoes, unfrayed socks, and run-free stockings. Good grooming is simply good self-maintenance. We are expected, by the way, to do that maintenance—including makeup—in private. The clipping of nails at the office desk and on public transportation has unfortunately become rather common. Horror stories of workplace incivility include toothbrushing at the office drinking fountain.

Be ready to make little grooming-related sacrifices for the sake of those around you. If you carpool or use public transportation, don't wear strong perfume or aftershave lotions. You don't want to overwhelm your fellow riders. About perfumes in general, there are those who dislike them or are allergic to them. Make sure that your wearing perfume at work is not a problem for your coworkers.

After hours of teamwork at the office, you may just want to spend your next break doing nothing but relaxing. Be considerate and make yourself go and swish some mouthwash freshness into your breath before the break is over.

Your doctor will be exposed to parts of your naked body when he or she sees you for your checkup. If you don't feel clean after a day at work, go home to scrub and shower before your appointment. If this is impossible, clean yourself as best you can in your workplace bathroom. Make a mental note to better coordinate your commitments the next time.

It's Saturday morning and you are not planning to go out all day. Do you *have* to shave? Do you *have* to wash your hair? Do you *have* to wear clean underwear even if that means doing a load of laundry because your underwear drawer is empty? Maybe you *want* to shave, wash your hair, and wear clean underwear, because you wouldn't be comfortable otherwise. But you may need an incentive. If it's hard to do the grooming just for yourself, do it for those who share your home. No one will be physically closer to you for a longer time than your companion, your spouse, and your family. Make sure that your body care is such that it adds to their pleasure in being with you. Let's disabuse ourselves of the rather common notion that although we are expected to be well groomed in public, there is nothing wrong with a little private slovenliness. This is part of a larger assumption that good manners may be forgotten when we are with those closest to us. On the contrary, being civil to them is one of the most concrete ways to show them that we love them. Love is not simply made of *feeling*. Real love is made of *doing*.

When we are well groomed, we often experience a sense of both physical and psychological well-being. We feel good, and we feel good about ourselves. When this happens, we are better disposed toward others, treat them better, and are thus better treated in return.

MINDING YOUR BODY BEYOND GOOD GROOMING

The civility of body management is more than good grooming habits. Here are some other civil ways to deal with our bodies that are equally important:

- Keep your fingers at a safe distance from your mouth, ears, and nose. You may think that the food you are eating is finger-licking good. This doesn't allow you to dramatize the cliché in front of your dinner companions, at the risk of eliciting justified twinges of disgust. If your fingers are sticky with food, wipe them with a napkin or wash your hands. Don't use your fingers to dislodge food from your teeth; what you need instead is a toothbrush and a bathroom. Don't stick a finger in your ear to collect anything, real or imaginary. If your ears need care, use Q-Tips or wax-removing tools in the privacy of your bathroom. Never stick your fingers up your nose. Simple and quick nose cleaning may be done wherever you are with the help of a handkerchief or a tissue. More elaborate nose care is done in private. As for nose blowing, do it quickly and unobtrusively. Afterward, don't check the handkerchief's contents as if—to use the vivid image found in medieval and Renaissance courtesy tracts—you expected pearls and precious stones to have fallen from your brain.

- Keep your mouth closed at all times while chewing. This, of course, means that you shouldn't talk and chew at the same time. Don't make any noises with your mouth. No slurping, no audible chewing, no smacking of the lips. Cover your mouth with your hand when yawning, coughing, or sneezing. The best way of handling a sneeze, however, is with the help of a handkerchief or a tissue.

- Don't sniffle, snort, or make any other unpleasant and annoying noise with your nose or your throat.

- Head for the bathroom whenever intestinal gas becomes a problem. Always wash your hands thoroughly on your way out.

- Never spit. Be careful not to spray those around you as you speak. If you speak at length (giving a presentation, for instance), unobtrusively wipe your mouth with a clean handkerchief once in a while. You will thus eliminate any unsightly buildup at the corners of your mouth.

- Don't scratch yourself. Don't chew your fingernails.

GOING ONE STEP BEYOND
THE GOLDEN RULE

WHATEVER I JUDGE REASONABLE OR UNREASONABLE THAT ANOTHER SHOULD DO FOR ME, THAT BY THE SAME JUDGMENT I DECLARE REASONABLE OR UNREASONABLE THAT I IN LIKE CASE SHOULD DO FOR HIM. AND TO DENY THIS EITHER IN WORK OR ACTION IS AS IF A MAN SHOULD CONTEND THAT THOUGH TWO AND THREE ARE EQUAL TO FIVE, YET THREE AND TWO ARE NOT SO. *—Samuel Clarke*

I gave my six students the go-ahead. As they hunched over their final exams, the gentle shuffling of sheets was the only noticeable noise in the classroom. Then one of the students—Chris—sniffled. And he sniffled again, loud and clear. And again. Having waited for several minutes, hoping in vain that a Kleenex would appear on the scene, I was presented with a dilemma. On the one hand, I wanted my class to be spared a distraction that threatened to go on indefinitely. This meant I would have to tell Chris to stop sniffling. On the other, I didn't want to hurt Chris's feelings. After a while, an idea came to me that seemed brilliant at the time. I would just give Chris a gentle hint. I went to the men's room, where I found what I needed. "You seem to have a nasty cold. Maybe you can use this," I whispered when I returned, while placing on his chair's armrest a cup of water and a piece of paper towel. Chris thanked me, drank from the cup, and politely dabbed his mouth with the towel I had hoped he would put to quite a different use. The failure of my nudging struck me as comical but also made me think. I immediately realized how I should have handled the little crisis. I should have asked Chris to please follow me into the hall, and there, out of the hearing range of the other students, I should have asked him, with all the tact at my disposal, to please blow his nose, for everybody's sake. Quite apart from this, however, it occurred to me that there was a serious lesson in the silly incident.

I knew Chris. It was not that he didn't care about breaking the concentration of his fellow students. He was kind and considerate. Had I had been frank with him, he would have blushed, apologized, and put an end to his sniffling right away. He simply hadn't been aware of his sniffling, or if he had, it hadn't occurred to him that it could be a problem. The sniffling of others probably didn't bother him, so he didn't think that his sniffling could bother others. All of this made me think of the Golden Rule.

That we should treat others the way we like others to treat us is a foundation of ethical thinking today as it was thousands of years ago. The Golden Rule works well and often because we all have similar basic needs and preferences. We all like it when others are hospitable to us, so it makes sense to be hospitable to them. We all dislike it when we are the victims of malicious gossip, so we know we shouldn't gossip maliciously. We all like it when people are sincere to us, so it's clear that lying is bad. And so on. But we also have standards and sensitivities that differ from those of others. I may be bothered by things (sniffling, for instance) you may not even notice, and vice versa. The Golden Rule tells us how to treat each other justly, but because it hinges upon the subjective, it is not always totally reliable. We should learn to respect others on their own terms as well. This means—to go back to my example one last time—being aware that others may be annoyed by our sniffling even though we don't find sniffling annoying at all. When we expand our awareness of the standards of others, we expand the best part of our soul. We are at our best when we go one step beyond the Golden Rule.

12. Be Agreeable

IF YOU WOULD BE LOVED, LOVE AND BE LOVABLE.

—*Benjamin Franklin*

I DO NOT WANT PEOPLE TO BE VERY AGREEABLE, AS IT SAVES ME THE TROUBLE OF LIKING THEM A GREAT DEAL.

—*Jane Austen*

Do you know people who are incapable or unwilling to harmonize their needs and preferences with those of others—even their closest friends? I do, and I am both fascinated and put off by them. I am put off by them for the same reason most people are: chronic dissenters are a tiresome bunch. I am fascinated by them because they seem to be at ease with their own inflexibility. I'm the opposite, probably to a fault. I'm made uneasy by conflicts big and small, and I'm happiest when I can easily agree, especially with those closest to me. Compromise is not a dirty word in my book. So I inevitably look with puzzled awe at those who seem to thrive on confrontation and disagreement. I'm not speaking of political dissent here or fighting for just causes. I'm speaking instead of an inclination to disregard others' desires in everyday occurrences.

- Rachel, Taniyka, Ramona, and Sally are planning their monthly girls-only after-work dinner. A few minutes into the discussion a consensus seems to emerge. As Rachel suggests a new restaurant that has received excellent reviews, Ramona interjects that she, too, has heard of the restaurant's wonderful Moroccan dishes. "Sounds exciting," says Taniyka. "I'm game." Now it's Sally's turn to chime in. Although she has nothing against Moroccan cuisine, she vetoes the others' choice. The restaurant is no good because it has no outdoor dining. Her three friends reply that it's still early in the season for eating outside—in fact, it's downright chilly—so the new Moroccan restaurant sounds really good. Sally, however, knows what she wants and won't budge.

- On their first full day in Paris, Louise and her husband, Herb, join their good friends Lana, Bob, Karen, and John, with whom they are vacationing in Europe. "Time to see some churches," says John. "Anybody interested?" It turns out that almost everybody is. Only Herb happens not to be in the mood for art and architecture. He wants to shop for a sports coat. Although Louise would like to join the group, it's also important for her to share her day's experiences in Paris with her husband. "Why don't we all go see the sights together today," she suggests to him, "and tomorrow I'll go shopping with you?" But Herb doesn't seem to understand or care. He won't change his mind no matter what anybody else—his wife included—wants or intends to do.

- Ted and Terrence are teaching assistants at a liberal arts college. They both teach an undergraduate introductory class twice a week. For the last two years Ted has taught the Tuesday-Thursday section and Terrence the Monday-Wednesday one. They have gotten used to their routine and look forward to a few more years of the same. Ted's wife's difficult pregnancy, however, changes everything. Now it would be much more convenient for him to teach the Monday-Wednesday section. He explains the situation to Terrence, hoping that he will be willing to switch sessions with him. Terrence doesn't see why his routine should be disrupted. He likes it just the way it is. Why should he be penalized for being single? His answer is no.

Now, Sally, Herb, and Terrence are entitled to their own preferences. None of them is guilty of major wrongdoing. And yet more flexibility would certainly make them more endearing. We are not expected to comply with the preferences of others in every situation of our lives. That would be absurd, not civil. However, civility mandates that we at least make an effort to harmonize our plans with those of others whenever we have no compelling reasons not to do so. *Whenever* is key here: agreeing once in a blue moon—and maybe begrudgingly—doesn't make you an agreeable person.

One major area of everyday life to grace with agreeableness is that of conversation. Respect for others entails having an essentially welcoming attitude toward the words they address to us. This means, among other things, that contradicting for its own sake should be banned as utterly uncivil. There are two fundamental abilities to cultivate in order to be agreeable in conversation.

• The ability to consider that you might be wrong.

• The ability to admit that you don't know.

At any given moment, on any issue, there is the possibility that you might be wrong and someone else might be right. Keep that possibility in mind. Then, if you realize that you *are* wrong, find the strength to acknowledge it openly. Do so graciously, without harboring resentment toward the person who happens to be right. The same awareness and openness apply to not knowing. We are not omniscient and nobody expects us to be. So, reconcile yourself with not knowing and admit that fact to your interlocutors. Training yourself to consider that you might be wrong and to admit that you don't know will mark a crucial point in your relationships. Accepting those limitations about yourself will make you much more accepting of others. You will listen to learn rather than to react and you will be less likely to attack, to be dismissive, to doubt good intentions, and to be dogmatic.

One of the most important things you can do to improve your relationships—both in your private life and at work—is listen to agree. Again, I am not saying that you *have* to agree with whatever is being said (see the rule "Assert Yourself"). Rather, I am encouraging you to look for possibilities of agreement. Condition yourself to recognize similarities between your views and those of others. Very often we do just the opposite: we emphasize our differences in order to strengthen our identities and show our independence. Sometimes we need to do that, but most of the time we don't. We may feel good about ourselves doing it, without realizing that we are alienating our interlocutors. Keeping an open mind is a good starting point for the building of meaningful connections. We should, however, make the further effort of identifying and pursuing points of agreement in the myriad of words that are addressed to us every day.

Following the advice of age-old wisdom, choose your battles. Fight only those that *need* to be fought and steer clear of all others. Think of all the physical and nervous energy that an inane argument requires. Ask yourself: "Do I want to engage in this argument? Is there a compelling reason to do so? Am I being strong or weak by doing it? Am I championing a valid cause or am I just being defensive?" We often entangle ourselves in disputation just because we are afraid that if we don't, someone else will look good—not the noblest of reasons, to be sure. So, show your strength: let others shine. That's being agreeable.

We need agreement in our lives because it is gratifying and healing, because human bonds could not be forged without it, and because it is the foundation of social harmony. Of course disagreement can be productive. "A little rebellion, now and then, is a good thing," observed Thomas Jefferson. In disagreement alone, however, we couldn't survive. In ordinary circumstances—at home, at work, at school, in traffic, at the grocery store, in a restaurant, at the mall, at the library, in church, on a bus, in a doctor's office, or inside a crowded elevator—we can make a positive difference in the life of others (and in our own) by just being pleasant to them. One essential way of being pleasant is being agreeable. Plentiful rewards await those who manage to be just that.

ON SAYING YES TO CIVILITY

Another way of being agreeable is saying yes to civility. By allowing others to be civil—and thus pleasant—to us, we please them. Whenever possible, let's say yes (and thank you) when others offer us the gift of their regard, kindness, and consideration. By accepting, we reward the giver. We often decline kind offers because we don't want to inconvenience the other person, because of excessive pride, because we lack self-esteem (we don't think we deserve the attention), or because we feel we are losing control. But others need to give us their kindness as much as we need to receive and treasure it.

As you say good-bye to your friend, he hands you his spare umbrella, telling you that he doesn't need it. Consider taking it, even if you are thinking that your raincoat may give you enough protection from the drizzle. Walking your dog on a hot summer day, you stop to exchange a few words with an older neighbor relaxing in his yard. He volunteers to get a bowl of water for your panting puppy. Even though you are almost home, you may want to say yes. Tending to a thirsty puppy (and petting him) might make your kind neighbor's day. Noticing that you look tired after a grueling week at work, your wife tells you to take the passenger's, rather than your usual driver's, seat for the three-hour drive to your weekend destination. Don't fight her good intention.

Let's learn how to give. But let's also become proficient in the difficult art of receiving.

13. Keep It Down
(and Rediscover Silence)

Kendall, that's *not* your inside voice," the father of the sprightly four-year-old quietly but firmly observed. "That's your *outside* one." Little Kendall, whom Mother Nature had provided with powerful vocal cords, immediately switched to the appropriate, lower register. Sensitive as I am to the scourge of unnecessary and unwanted noise, I felt like breaking into applause and bestowing exuberant praise upon both parent and child. Yes, I told myself, the virtue of moderation in noise production was being kept alive for the new generations. There *was* hope after all.

Noise is among the most pervasive and frustrating sources of everyday annoyance—and sometimes a veritable pain. Careful management of noise is a must for those who want to be civil. Why is noise pollution so prevalent? Because many don't seem to see (or rather *hear*) the problem at all and many of those who do don't care enough to correct it. The practicing piano virtuoso transported by his own music may forget that his neighbors' bedroom is only a few inches from his thundering instrument. A late-night reveler may be aware of but dismiss as inconsequential the discomfort his loud merrymaking inflicts upon others. Irrespective of the different mind-sets, in either case somebody's peace is unnecessarily disturbed. In either case, sensitivity (or, if you prefer, civility) should have prevailed.

Don't pummel those who live with and around you with loud sounds coming from your television, computer, and CD player. Make sure you don't schedule noisy lawn mowing and leaf blowing before nine o'clock in the morning. Abstain from frivolous honking. Your car horn is neither for saying hello nor for venting your frustration. Use it only to increase road safety. Headphones are a must when listening to music on public transportation.

Respect silence in houses of worship. The chatter of rude adults and the whining and screaming of tired or unruly small children can spoil a religious service. We seem to be forgetting today that libraries call for a quiet demeanor. In a library, converse only in the designated group-study areas. In a restaurant, keep your voice down, just like at the office. In a theater, don't speak at all. You may have noticed that some food critics rate restaurants not only in the categories of food and atmosphere but also in that of quiet. A noise meter is part of today's sophisticated restaurant reviewer's professional kit.

Before entering houses of worship, libraries, restaurants, and theaters, turn off your cellular telephone. For incoming emergency calls, switch your pagers to vibrating mode. In general, your telephone should be turned off whenever its ringing would distract or annoy others. This includes all of your meetings, whether work-related or social.

If you go to the movies (or to live plays, the opera, or concerts), sooner or later you will have to deal with the chattering of fellow audience members. Can you live with it? If not, try first an inquisitive glance and then a polite whisper: "Excuse me, but your talking makes it difficult for me to enjoy the show." Should this fail, don't repeat your plea. You want to prevent the incident from escalating. And you want to be considerate of those who are not sitting close enough to be bothered by the chatter but would certainly notice an altercation. At this point, change seats, if you can, or bring the matter to the attention of an usher or a supervisor.

The strategy remains the same when dealing with noise polluters of all stripes. Decide how much you are willing to tolerate. Should you choose to intervene, take a big breath and remind yourself to remain clearheaded. Explain to the offender what the noise does to you and make your polite but firm request. Just as you don't want to be driven by your own anger, work hard at keeping the anger of others down. To do this, avoid accusatory tones and impress upon the other person that you are confident that the two of you can ultimately reach an agreement. If it feels right, propose or accept a reasonable compromise. The alternative is to seek a resolution with the help of a mediator.

In an age when background noises are virtually constant, we are slowly becoming inured to noise.

LET US BE SILENT—SO WE MAY HEAR THE WHISPER OF THE GODS.   *—Ralph Waldo Emerson*

At the same time, many of us are ready to reacquaint ourselves with silence. We are beginning to realize that silence is not a void waiting to be filled, just as an immaculate church wall is not there to be defaced with spray paint. Silence is not necessarily the sign of a failure to communicate. Instead, it can be the refreshing result of a choice. We often surround ourselves with chatter and sundry sounds because we don't want to be alone with our thoughts. While noise takes us away from ourselves, through silence we build bridges to our own souls. Ultimately, the challenge to all of us on the threshold of the new century (which threatens to be a noisy one) is to treat silence as an endangered precious resource. There is an urgent need for advocates of silence. There is an urgent need for gatherers of tranquillity.

ECOLOGISTS OF QUIET

While celebrating International Noise Awareness Day in 2001, Les Blomberg observed that "our soundscape is like our landscape in that noise is to that soundscape as litter is to the landscape, and . . . we've really cluttered up our soundscape and it's time to start cleaning it up." Les Blomberg is executive director of the Noise Pollution Clearinghouse, an organization of ecologists of quiet whose motto is "Good neighbors keep their noise to themselves." The Clearinghouse's mission is "to create more civil cities and more natural rural and wilderness areas by reducing noise pollution at the source." Hearing loss, stress, and high blood pressure are among the consequences of noise pollution. Experimental studies have also shown that noise has negative effects on children's learning and on performance in the workplace. "Friends of quiet," wrote Mr. Blomberg, "need to be part Rachel Carson and part Miss Manners. We need to demand that common property be protected, that our air remains clean, free of noise, smog, acid rain, etc., and that others be treated respectfully and in a manner we would wish for ourselves."

14. Respect Other People's Time

ALL THAT TIME IS LOST WHICH MIGHT BE BETTER EMPLOYED.
                                        —*Jean-Jacques Rousseau*

DOST THOU LOVE LIFE? THEN DO NOT SQUANDER TIME; FOR
THAT'S THE STUFF LIFE IS MADE OF.   —*Benjamin Franklin*

We respect other people's time when we learn to value it as much as our own. Even better, we can get to a point where we won't distinguish between our time and the time of others. We then respect time as such—as the precious commodity it is—and act upon this respect in every situation. This does not mean having a constant preoccupation with time. It is possible to make an automatic appreciation of time part of who we are and still go through life at an unhurried pace.

Punctuality is nonnegotiable. Arriving on time is a basic rule of considerate behavior. When you happen to be more than five minutes late, call. Of course, you should try to arrange your schedule realistically, so that a delay will be unlikely. It is not civil to schedule your day's appointments knowing in advance that you will be late for one or maybe all of them. To cancel a lunch date—or any other kind of appointment—at the last moment is also rude. These actions show that you are more than willing to inconvenience others when this best suits your plans. This is wrong because it's unfair. Consider every appointment a commitment to be there and to be there at the agreed-upon time. If you have agreed a minute ago to call upon your friend *at* ten the next morning, don't say, just before you go, "So, I'll see you *around* ten." This tells your friend that you are already taking your commitment lightly and managing time according to your own convenience. When you say ten, mean ten.

A telephone call is a demand for attention and time that can occur at inconvenient times. Consider opening your calls by asking, "Am I disturbing you?" Keep your calls short, especially if you have the impression that the other person is busy. Brevity is also in order when calling from a public telephone, calling from someone else's home or office, or calling someone who is in someone else's home or office. If you anticipate a lengthy call, ask whether this is a good time to talk.

As a rule, your machine should answer for you only when you are not present to take your calls. Keep exceptions to a minimum. If you can, make same-day return calls, whether they are personal or business-related.

> CALL WAITING TITILLATES THE BASEST OF IMPULSES—GREED AND OPPORTUNISM. (SO SORRY, A SUBSEQUENT ENGAGEMENT, AS OSCAR WILDE PROPHETICALLY SAID.) IT PLAYS ON OUR ANXIETY—THE NASTY LITTLE NEED TO KNOW WHAT OR WHO MIGHT BE BETTER THAN WHAT WE'VE GOT NOW.
> —*Lynne Sharon Schwartz*

Use call-waiting as infrequently as possible. Only an emergency justifies a sudden taking leave of someone so that you can direct your attention to someone else. Should this happen, return to the previous call in a matter of seconds and apologize for the interruption.

Whether you are in a store or an office, demanding immediate attention is uncivil and ineffective. By waiting your turn you don't waste the time and energies of those whose job is to help you. The quality of their work will be better and so will the quality of life of all involved. Of course, if you realize that you are being ignored, speak up—firmly and politely. In your workplace, try to be brief and clear as you communicate with your coworkers. Openly share with them what you know, so that they can fully benefit from it and save time. Always respect deadlines upon which you have agreed.

Be careful not to hold your friends hostage. You may expect that they will devote some time to your problems; the demand for time you are imposing on them, however, should be reasonable. State the essentials of the problem, elicit their reactions or advice, if that's what you want, but don't expect hours of commiseration. Pay attention to your friends' hints that they want to put an end to the meeting. "I really, *really* have to go now" means: "You made me stay longer than I wanted." It also means that you should have been more sensitive to *their* needs.

A FINAL OBSERVATION

Always give others the amount of time that they can rightfully expect from you. Don't cut short a scheduled meeting on a whim or just because it's convenient for you. The other persons may need all of the scheduled time to make their point or to fully evaluate your position. They may have made a considerable effort to find the time for the meeting and to reach the meeting place. Allow them to feel that they have accomplished all that they could. Cutting the meeting short for your own self-serving purposes may cause disappointment, irritation, and frustration.

15. Respect Other People's Space

One of the most elementary ways of being considerate is by respecting personal space. Leave enough room between yourself and others so that they won't feel uncomfortable or intimidated. The fervor of your convictions gives you no license to sermonize in another's face. Standing at an appropriate distance from others is part of poise, which gives strength and authority to your words. If the elevator you have been eagerly awaiting arrives at your floor looking like an open can of sardines, keep waiting. You may be in a hurry, but you don't want to make everybody's ride even more uncomfortable.

Pay attention to others' reactions to the way you manage space in conversation. By taking a step back, the other person may be letting you know that you are standing too close. Do respect the new distance between the two of you, rather than unthinkingly take a step forward. Codes of personal space vary from culture to culture. For Southern Europeans, Latin Americans, and Arabs, for instance, sitting, standing, and walking only a few inches from one another is seldom a problem. Northern Europeans and many North Americans, however, need more personal space to feel at ease. So, when in Rome . . . at least be aware that personal space may be measured differently than at home.

Many people touch others as they converse with them. Although there is no excuse for grabbing, a squeeze of a hand, an arm, or a shoulder is acceptable, depending on the circumstances. At work, it's a good idea to keep touching to a minimum. As you allow more room for spontaneity in your personal life, don't assume that every friend or acquaintance will be at ease with physical contact. To many people, being touched feels like a violation of personal space. Pay attention to others' reactions to your touching and stop at the first sign of uneasiness. In turn, make others aware of how you feel about being touched. If they can't read your body language or won't pay attention to it, tell them.

Respect that extension of personal space some call territory. Our home is our territory, and so is our office at work or the space we have claimed for our family on the beach on a sunny summer day. Our territory is any space we are entitled to control. The stranger who comes to sit at my table in a crowded cafeteria without asking whether I mind is violating my territory. The deliveryman who lets himself into my office without knocking on the door first (it happened twice in the last several months, by the way) is doing the same. And so is the driver who tailgates me when I'm on my way home from the office. In different ways, they show a lack of respect for a space that should be mine. By extension, they don't respect me. They are all acting rudely. The only difference is that the tailgater is also a threat to the lives of others. That's incivility with a vengeance.

Sometimes we make it difficult or impossible for others to have access to space that they should be able to claim without hassle. I must confess I have often placed my briefcase on the seat next to mine on a train, hoping to discourage other travelers from occupying it. If that's not rude, it's at least not very nice. What is certainly rude, however, is to position your car so that it occupies two parking spaces instead of one. I may be wrong, but it seems to me that this is happening more frequently than it used to. Unauthorized parking in the spaces for the handicapped is a similar breach of civility that seems to be on the rise. There is simply no excuse for it.

Respect for others' territory at home is a sound foundation for good relationships. We all have parts of our homes we consider our own more than others—maybe a bedroom, a study, a closet, a bathroom, a workstation, or a workshop in a corner of the garage. It is not unreasonable to expect that those who live with us will leave those spaces as undisturbed as possible. Nobody should barge into any bedroom or bathroom that others use as well. Children five years and older should always ask permission to enter their parents' bedroom even if the door is open. Living rooms, family rooms, and kitchens are everybody's space. Anybody needing exclusive use of them for a considerable amount of time ought to make sure that's not a problem for the other members of the household. In general, whenever you are at home, make sure that you are not interfering with what others are doing at that very moment. Exercise good judgment regarding when to bring friends into the home and how long they should remain. Throughout their stay you are responsible for making sure that they are not loud, intrusive, or disruptive.

Respecting others' territory at work is also a must. Make it part of your professional identity. Office space today often knows no doors and is framed by shoulder-high partitions rather than walls. Because privacy is so difficult to obtain, we are all expected to make a valiant effort to be discreet. Keep your voice low, whether you are speaking with someone present or on the telephone. Use a conference room for teamwork or if you have visitors. Shouting between cubicles is intrusive and annoying. Whenever you need to talk to coworkers, either call them on the telephone, e-mail them, or get up and walk. Don't just step into their cubicles with your problem at the ready, however, but rather ask if you may come in and if they have time to talk. Should the other person be on the telephone at the time of your arrival, don't hover, but rather leave and come back later. Don't drop your purse, briefcase, or papers on your coworkers' workstations, and refrain from picking up and examining anything belonging to them.

COME NOT NEAR THE BOOKS OR WRITINGS OF ANOTHER SO AS TO READ THEM UNLESS DESIRED; ALSO LOOK NOT NIGH WHEN ANOTHER IS WRITING A LETTER.
—*George Washington*

Show no interest in your coworkers' faxes and sundry correspondence and don't let your glance rest on the e-mail message (or anything else, for that matter) they may have on their computer screen. Finally, unless it is common practice in your workplace to swap workstations, use your coworkers' only with their permission or if instructed to do so by your boss. When you are finished, leave everything as you found it, adding just a thank-you note with the day and times of your presence there. People exiting elevators take precedence over people entering them. The same threshold etiquette applies to the entering and exiting from buildings, stores, offices, and rooms of all kinds. Anyone stepping out ought to be allowed to do so before anyone else steps in. It is a logical sequence of space management: first comes the vacating, then the filling.

When waiting for your table in a restaurant, don't hover over the tables of others. Should you spot people you know, you may stop at their table for a greeting, but don't invite yourself to join them. If they invite you and you are comfortable with the unplanned arrangement, go ahead and accept. When the people you know are in the company of people you don't know, acknowledge them with just a nod or a "Hello" as you walk to your table. Don't stop and linger at their table in the hope that introductions will be made. It is up to your acquaintances or friends to give you a clear indication that they want you to stop and chat.

Respect the privacy of the strangers sitting at neighboring tables. Refrain from insinuating yourself into their conversation. ("I'm a patient of Dr. Burger's myself! Isn't she a wonderful woman?") It is not appropriate to ask them what they think of this or that dish on the menu, nor should you volunteer your opinions on the food. Finally, keep your little children from wandering to the tables of other diners.

A FEW MORE WORDS ON CIVILITY IN THE WORKPLACE

One key measure of our satisfaction at work is the quality of the relationships we have with our coworkers. Good relationships contribute to keeping stress down. This is a blessing in an environment where the sources of stress are manifold and often difficult to eliminate. It seems likely that workplace climate issues will become increasingly prominent in the next several years. Simply put: We are going to be more and more aware of the toll that work-related stress takes on us. And we will become more and more willing to do something about it. What does this mean? Let's consider the quandary millions of workers are facing today.

Today's workers are aware of the possibility that their retirement may start later than they anticipated. This is owing, in part, to the fact that Social Security and medical costs increase with an increased life expectancy. Workers may have to work more to finance their longer lives. At the same time, the increase in workplace stress caused in part by a prevalent strategy of cost reductions makes retirement more appealing. Many workers want to retire sooner than anticipated.

We are facing a conflict, then, between the need to stay on the job for a longer time than anticipated and the inclination to quit sooner. It's not unreasonable to predict that lower-stress workplaces—workplaces, that is, where civility makes for better relationships among coworkers—will become very appealing. These are the workplaces where organizations will manage to attract and retain an increasing number of first-rate workers. This should be a strong incentive for organizations to promote a culture of civility in their workplaces.

16 . Apologize Earnestly

MOST APOLOGIES ARE GESTURES OF EMPATHY; THEY EXPRESS
REGRET FOR OFFENDING SOMEONE ELSE'S FEELINGS OR CON-
CERNS. APOLOGIZING IMPLIES THAT YOU ARE AWARE OF THE
FEELINGS OF ANOTHER AND CAN EMPATHIZE SUFFICIENTLY TO
REGRET HAVING INJURED THAT PERSON.   —*Daniel Jankelovich*

Apologizing is a decent thing to do, but it is not true that the
more we do it the better human beings we are. As we become
more aware of the needs of others and more willing to honor them,
we find ourselves apologizing less frequently. That's because we
prevent mistakes from happening rather than manage them after
they have occurred. Perfection not being of this world, however,
apologies remain one of the most valuable resources of the fair and
the considerate.

When we apologize, we acknowledge that we did something
wrong and work at repairing the damage. Apologies should be
thoughtfully conceived, clearly stated, and heartfelt. They need not
be long and elaborate but should convey that we know exactly
what we did that was wrong, that we understand the *effects* of our
actions, and that we are not looking for *excuses*.

The elderly woman on crutches had been laboriously approaching the door of the store for the last few minutes. From the op-

posite direction, a woman with a jittery dog straining at a long leash was quickly nearing. The dog barked and lunged at the elderly woman, who recoiled, struggling to keep her balance. Only then, when the dog was a few inches from her crutches, did the other woman pull on the leash, calling the dog's name. With touching sweetness, the elderly woman said, "That's all right, as long as he doesn't get to me." The dog lunged and barked again. The other woman said, "He has never seen crutches before," and briskly walked away.

The woman with the dog might have felt a twinge of regret seeing the old woman coming close to falling. However, a simple apology was in order (such as "I'm sorry; I should have kept him on a shorter leash"), not an explanation—certainly not one shifting the responsibility for the incident. She ignored the fact that she should have had better control of her dog. Instead, she essentially faulted the elderly woman for being on crutches.

Apologizing is one thing; exculpating yourself is quite another: don't mix the two. The woman with the dog did just that. This muddying of the waters of apology is common. How many times do we hear pseudo-apologies such as: "I'm sorry I yelled at you on the phone, but I'm under a lot of stress these days"? This is how a *real* apology sounds: "I want to apologize for yelling at you. There is no excuse for that. I can only say that it won't happen again." Sometimes those who accept your apology will provide your excuse for you: "Apology accepted. I appreciate your saying that. We are all under a lot of stress these days." But they don't have to let you off the hook and you should not expect that they will.

An honest evaluation of a complaint will make you decide whether apologies are in order. If you believe that you are at fault, apologize in earnest. Expressions such as "I know how you feel," "I see where you're coming from," "I'm sorry you feel that way," and even "I'm trying to correct the situation" are other pseudo-apologies. They are frequently used in place of real apologies by those who refuse to take responsibility for their actions.

"Oh, I must go back to get something." The cashier at the grocery counter looked up as the woman who had spoken, whose items he was checking out, quickly disappeared in the direction of the aisles. A good three minutes later she was back with her new purchases. "I'm sorry; I appreciate your patience," she said to the shopper next to her in line, who had been waiting all the while.

Under the veneer of politeness, there was something uncomfortably disingenuous and rude in those words of apology. The woman knew that making everybody stop in their tracks for her convenience was wrong, but she did it anyway. Her apology rang hollow. A real apology is never a self-authorization to be inconsiderate. The woman's civil alternative would have been to let the cashier complete the checkout of the items she already had, then go back for those she had forgotten and stand in line at the checkout station again.

Why is it so difficult to apologize? Because to articulate an earnest apology we need to win a struggle with our own pride. Thinking that apologies put us in a position of weakness, we often wait for others to apologize first. When we bring ourselves to apologize, however, we discover how cathartic it is. It may be hard to believe, but I *like* to apologize. I enjoy it in the same way I enjoy paying my debts. It's a cleaning of the slate. Indeed, if you think of it, an apology is the payment of a moral debt. That's why we say, "I *owe* you an apology."

A final word of caution: Don't assume that your apology will be always and immediately well received. Especially if it was difficult for you to apologize, you may expect an automatic reward for your effort. Consider, then, that those you hurt may find it just as difficult to accept your apology. Your acknowledgment of your wrongdoing does not necessarily erase their hurt. They may need time to grant you the forgiveness you are, in effect, seeking. In that case, you can only accept the rejection and find comfort in the thought that you may try again under more favorable circumstances. Take your time, showing all the while that you have mended your ways.

17. Assert Yourself

THE ASSERTIVE PERSON STANDS UP FOR HER OWN RIGHTS AND EXPRESSES HER PERSONAL NEEDS, VALUES, CONCERNS, AND IDEAS IN DIRECT AND APPROPRIATE WAYS. WHILE MEETING HER OWN NEEDS, SHE DOES NOT VIOLATE THE NEEDS OF OTHERS OR TRESPASS ON THEIR PERSONAL SPACE.   *—Robert Bolton*

ASSERTIVENESS AND THE QUEST FOR MEANING GO HAND IN HAND.   *—Henry Dreher*

Wanting to please others is a noble sentiment at the root of civility and an indispensable ingredient in happy relationships. However, just as crucial for our happiness is the ability to establish firm personal boundaries.

I liked, I *loved,* my grandmother, who treated men and women's feelings as if they were made of brittle glass and who handled them with fine dextrous fingers. I like people who go slowly and feel their way and are discreet and careful of their words, people who move delicately and tread on no one's dreams. "Civilized" is my favorite word. That being so, how could I have lived for years with this man? And why can't I tell him to go away?

Mary, the protagonist of Ruth Rendell's novel *The Keys to the Street,* is a study in delicacy of body and soul.

> A GOOD REASON FOR NOT ASSERTING YOURSELF IS, OF
> COURSE, THAT YOU THINK YOU ARE NOT WORTH THE
> EFFORT! —*Gael Lindenfield*

Sensitive to the feelings of others but lacking in self-esteem, she cannot bring herself to utter the unequivocal words to end her relationship with her self-serving and abusive boyfriend. My dictionary lists "fineness of feeling with regard to what is fitting, proper, etc.," as one of the meanings of *delicacy*. The example accompanying that definition in the dictionary—"Delicacy would not permit her to be rude"—could be aptly used to describe Mary's feelings.

Mary's real problem, however, is that her submissive delicacy does not allow her to see that asserting herself would *not* be rude at all. She doesn't see that assertiveness ought to be a natural consequence of her being reasonably sensitive to her own needs. A healthy attention to our needs does not conflict with the principle of respect for persons upon which civility is built. There is no doubt in my mind that assertiveness is part of the set of quiet but powerful interactive skills of civility.

Like Mary, we all find at times that we are unable or unwilling to express what we need, believe, or want with the firmness that makes others take serious notice. It's not always easy telling the annoying coworker inquiring about our personal life to just stop, or turning down an invitation to a social event we don't really feel like attending, or sticking to the rule that we won't take work-related telephone calls at home—even important ones—or informing the couple we usually invite for Labor Day that this year we are making different plans with other friends. When we believe we are antagonizing or rejecting others we feel guilty toward *them* and apprehensive of the consequences *we* might endure. Will they still think that we like them? Will they still like us? Fearful and unsettled, instead of asserting ourselves we stumble, we mumble, we hesitate, we obfuscate, and we give in, needlessly adding frustration to our lives.

How do we unlearn these self-defeating ways? Let's take, for example, the "No" to the reception we don't feel like attending. This "No" to others is nothing but a "Yes" to ourselves and our needs. We can *choose* to say no because we are *entitled* to exercise control over our own expenditures of time and energy. It is *our* time; it is *our* energy; it ought to be *our* choice. By saying no to someone else and yes to ourselves, we aren't *taking* something that belongs to others; we are simply *keeping* something that is rightfully ours. This is commonsensical, and yet it takes practice to transform it into second nature.

The good news is that if you are serious about reprogramming yourself for assertiveness, in the end you will usually succeed. When you manage to say a good, solid, "Yes," to something you want or an equally powerful, "No," to something you don't, you experience a small (sometimes not so small) swell of elation. This comes from having identified what is right for you and bravely and successfully reached for it. You will want to enjoy this kind of victory over and over again. You will also be encouraged by the positive consequences of these victories. Assertiveness not only feels good but also works well.

Let's go back to our apprehension that by antagonizing our interlocutor we might jeopardize a relationship important to us. We rarely consider that if we fail to be assertive our relationships may be in danger just the same. Let's suppose that you have made it clear to those you invited to your fortieth birthday party that it's going to be open only to adults. And let's also suppose that one of your guests informs you of his intention to bring his two preteen children. Unwilling to antagonize your friend, you acquiesce, although you feel somewhat bullied and more than mildly resentful.

These feelings are perhaps a more serious threat to your relationship with your friend than anything a polite but frank "No" on your part might have stirred. Your submissive reaction may encourage your friend to disregard your legitimate wishes again in the future. This would increase the strain on your relationship. Thus assertiveness is undoubtedly the best option for all involved. Finding the strength to be assertive is handsomely rewarding. It will leave you at peace with yourself and increase the health of all your relationships.

A serious quarrel with your friend, spouse, or lover has left you angry and confused. He wants to make a hasty peace, relying on what seems to you a halfhearted apology. You, however, need more time to sort out how you really feel about what happened, and you tell him so. He pressures you to just forget what happened, arguing that it was not such a big thing after all. That makes you feel belittled and bullied, on top of everything else. Now you know: this is a time that calls for assertiveness. Your taking an assertive stance is clearly justified, and you are determined to make it work for you.

Here is how a strong and effective assertive message might sound: "When you tell me to just forget our fights, I feel upset because I'm not allowed to figure out with you why they really happened and we can't seek a real closure together." The three essential elements of a good assertion are all here: the description of the behavior you find objectionable, the disclosure of the feelings stirred in you by the behavior, and the naming of the behavior's effects.

Prepare yourself for a defensive response. It might be something along the lines of "You always blow things out of proportion. I said I'm sorry, didn't I? What do you want me to do? Why can't you just lighten up for a change?" Don't respond in kind. Stay away from counteraccusations and don't stray into debating other issues, such as your personality and attitudes. Say that you will be glad to address those issues another time, but for now you want to focus on your present concern and nothing else. Restate your concern. Usually the second time around all of us are more willing to *really* listen.

Many acts of assertion are often much simpler than the one just outlined. Becoming assertive means, to a large extent, learning to say no. And part of that is being aware that it is your privilege to keep your "No" simple and short. There is certainly no need to transform your straightforward expression of preference or need into a discussion.

- "Will you write a letter of recommendation for me?"
  "No, I don't think I should."

- "Will you invest in my dotcom company?"
  "No, but thank you for asking."

- "Will you help me write my paper?"
  "No, I don't think it's a good idea."

"No, thank you"; "No, I prefer not to"; "No, that's not what I had in mind"; "No, I can't do that for you"; "No, I'm not prepared to do that"; "No, I'm not comfortable with it." Any of these "No Phrases" should suffice, but of course there will be those who expect more. Regardless of others' reaction to your "No," in most everyday interactions you owe them no explanation. You may decide to volunteer one when dealing with close friends. No one, however—and especially not a friend—should force you to revise your decision or make you feel guilty for not disclosing your reasons. If your No Phrase doesn't discourage an obstinate and guilt-inducing interlocutor the first time you utter it, don't be afraid to repeat it. And repeat it. It's called the broken record strategy. It works.

Medical science tells us that nonassertive behavior is a health risk. Pioneering experimental work has documented that self-neglect and overcompliance can compromise the functioning of our immune system, leaving us more vulnerable to a number of diseases. In an illuminating book, Henry Dreher provides a survey of these scientific finds, focusing on the work of George Salomon. Dreher's conclusion is clear and empowering: "Every time you succeed in establishing a healthy boundary, taking a stand of self-protection, having your feelings heard, or eliciting respect for your autonomy, you rouse the deep part of yourself that feels worthy of selfhood. These actions and reflections . . . are not only a balm for our soul, they are a boon to our health."

ON CHILLING OUT

Do people respond to your remonstrations by observing that "it's no big deal"? Do you stand accused of "blowing things out of proportion"? Are you summarily advised to "lighten up" or "chill out"? Of course, there are times when chilling out is the right thing to do. But there are also many instances when others try to silence you in order to escape justified criticism of their actions. How can you respond to an unwelcome and self-serving invitation to chill out? More or less like this: "No, I'm not going to chill out, and I'm telling you why. By telling me to chill out you are saying that I'm overreacting, which is like saying that I shouldn't feel the way I feel. I hope you'll allow me to have my feelings and to express them the way I choose. Since I happen to feel strongly about this issue, there is no reason I should look the other way. I suggest that instead of making me feel bad about my reaction, you come to terms with the seriousness of your actions."

18. Avoid Personal Questions

The incomparable Judith Martin (aka Miss Manners) wonders in one of her books why a common, polite invitation such as "If there is anything you want to know, don't hesitate to ask" should make her nervous. It does, she decides, because many people are all too ready to ask indiscreet personal questions: "Of course you should hesitate. It should be a pause long enough to ask yourself, 'Is this any of my business? Could this question hurt the other person's feelings? Could it seem to suggest something offensive about that person?' " It is in this very hesitation, in this exercise of discretion, that civility resides.

Taboo questions continue to make the rounds, kept in business by our inexhaustible curiosity about the business of others. Most of them have to do with religion, politics, money, personal relationships, health, and physical appearance. Here is a selection of questions that, depending on the circumstances, many people perceive as intrusive:

- "Do you believe in God?" "Do you go to synagogue?" "Do you pray at regular hours?" "Are you a practicing Catholic?" "Is your child baptized?"

- "For whom did you vote?" "Are you a liberal?" "Are you a conservative?"

- "How much do you make?" "How much did it cost?" "Is it paid for?" "What's your monthly payment?" "What's your net worth?"

- "How old are you?" "Are you married?" "Have you ever been married?" "Do you date?" "Why not?" "Why didn't you have any children?" "Did the two of you have an affair?" "Are you pregnant?" "Are you living together?" "Why haven't you married yet?"

- "What are you seeing the doctor for?" "What kind of surgery did you have?" "Why are you so pale?" "Are you ill?" "Have you lost weight?" "Have you gained weight?" "How come?"

Most of us have parts of our lives that we want to shelter from casual disclosure. Thus privacy-probing questions like these can unsettle, embarrass, and sometimes even anger us. How are we to respond to intrusive questions? Civilly, of course. Idle curiosity or a penchant for malicious gossip is not necessarily what prompts them. Sometimes genuine concern and an innocent desire to get to know others can take objectionable forms. This doesn't mean, however, that we should let our less than tactful interlocutors define our boundaries on our behalf. Whenever we believe that our privacy is threatened, it is our privilege to object.

Here are a few formulas with which you can defend your privacy: "I don't feel comfortable talking about this," "This is too big a question to be quickly addressed right now," "This isn't the best time to discuss this topic," "Let's not talk about money, if you don't mind," "I prefer not to discuss personal matters," and "I'm sorry, but I don't see why you need to know." Every individual instance of intrusiveness comes with its own route of polite evasion. "It must cost a fortune," says a first-time guest in your house looking at your impressive antique print. If you're not ready to put a money tag on it, you have the choice of saying nothing at all or just observing: "Well, I guess there aren't many of them around anymore." "How often does your cleaning woman come to clean your house?" a too-inquisitive neighbor wants to know. "Oh, as often as necessary," is an apt and polite reply.

A couple of weeks after we had put our house on the market, the telephone rang. Since it was late afternoon—prime telemarketing time—we braced for one more unwelcome sales pitch. This time it was the XYZ Moving and Storage Company. "Are you still planning to move?" asked the sales person without preamble. That a perfect stranger out of the blue should breezily ask her such question appalled Virginia. Answering that our plans were our business and nobody else's, she put an end to the call.

Now, I know that if the caller had started by saying "Good afternoon, Ms. Forni. We saw the listing of your home and were wondering if we may send you some information on our moving and storage services," Virginia's response would have been quite different. Notice that in this hypothetical version no direct question appears. The XYZ company never had a chance of getting our business. A rude ineptitude in communicating put it immediately out of contention.

A question that offends if asked out of the blue by a stranger may be acceptable when it comes from a friend or relative. It may also be acceptable if you have given the other person a clear indication of your willingness to speak of personal matters. Even so, refraining from asking direct personal questions is always a prudent and tactful option. In the natural process of getting acquainted, becoming friends, and strengthening our friendships, personal questions have a way of being answered even when they are not explicitly asked. Your interlocutor will volunteer information about his or her life when the time is right. So, be a thoughtful acquaintance and a loyal friend; show a nonintrusive interest in the other person, and give your relationship time to progress. The answers will follow of their own accord.

Don't be afraid that refraining from asking personal questions will cramp your conversation. It is a bad conversationalist who finds no other way of keeping the conversation alive than by asking intrusive questions. A good conversationalist makes the most of the information his or her companions volunteer. Ask questions that are not unduly personal and at the same time of real interest to you. If someone told you a story from his or her long-gone soldiering days, you might ask him or her what it was like being in the army back then. If you were introduced to a dog breeder, you might show an interest in the challenges of dog breeding today. Someone who told you she once was a nun probably won't mind being asked what she found appealing in the religious life. Having paid the right amount of attention to the other person's experiences, you may want to make a connection with your own. Maybe you were in the army, too. Maybe a book on dog breeds was a favorite of yours when you were a child. Maybe you are discovering that as you advance in years spirituality seems to matter more. There is always a way to pursue a genuine interest in others.

A couple of final notes. First, seeking permission to ask an intrusive question doesn't make your question any less intrusive. Before asking someone else, "May I ask you a personal question?"

ask yourself if there is a compelling reason for addressing a topic that can make the other person uncomfortable and for appearing eager to lift the screen of his or her privacy. Second, we can be intrusive not only by eliciting information about others but also by volunteering information about ourselves. The stranger you just met doesn't need to know whether your pregnancy was planned or the amount of your recent pay raise. This kind of information presumes a close relationship. One way to respect others is by being discreet about our own personal matters.

IS THAT AN ACCENT I DETECT?

"You have an accent. Where are you from?" After living for almost a quarter of a century in the United States, I still encounter this question. I usually don't mind. Sometimes I ask people to guess (Sweden, Poland, France, Holland, Great Britain, and Germany are the most common guesses, all wrong). I cannot say, however, that I am completely nonchalant when facing this inquiry.

For many nonnative speakers their accent is a serious matter, and they don't like being asked about it over and over again. They object to what they perceive as an unwarranted (even if unintentional) criticism of their linguistic abilities. They feel that no matter what they do to blend in, they will always be outsiders. Or, whatever the reason, they prefer not to release information about their background. As a general rule, I suggest that you avoid remarking about others' accents. Don't take the compliment route. Compliments on accents ("It's so nice," "It's so musical," "It's so exotic") often sound patronizing.

Accent aside, always use restraint when it comes to satisfying your curiosity about others' ethnic identity. People may be proud of being Hispanic, Arab, African or Native American, but may also resent off-the-cuff inquiries about "what" they are. They may think that you want to classify them rather than making the effort to deal with them as individuals. There is nothing wrong in your interest in their origins, but tact should prevail. Instead of asking them to present their ethnic credentials up front, let that information come forward within the natural progress of the conversation or of the relationship.

19. Care for Your Guests

WHAT IS PLEASANTER THAN THE TIE OF HOST AND GUEST?

—Aeschylus

YOU OUGHT TO MAKE WELCOME THE PRESENT GUEST, AND
SEND FORTH THE ONE WHO WISHES TO GO. *—Homer*

I know hospitality. In my youth I had the good fortune of being
the frequent guest of good people for whom having friends in the
house was as natural as breathing. The youngest of their three sons
was my best friend, and I practically grew up in their house. I was
such a fixture there that Signora Giovanna would introduce me to
her acquaintances by saying nonchalantly: "And this is my fourth
son." Not once was she other than motherly and kind to me. Not
once did she or her husband make me feel I wasn't welcome. They
gave me a sense of belonging and made me feel important. I know
now that was an injection of self-esteem I badly needed, and I'm
fairly certain that its good effects are still with me even after all
these years.

Not all hosts find themselves in the position of being such a
wonderful influence on their guests. There is truth, however, in
Anthelme Brillat-Savarin's remark that "to entertain a guest is to
make yourself responsible for his happiness." Certainly you want

your guests to have the best and the most comfortable of times. Commit yourself to their well-being, keeping in mind that sometimes small details make the difference. An end-of-the-meal announcement such as "I can make coffee or tea, if you want" may elicit polite refusals from those who don't want to trouble you. By saying instead: "I'm making coffee and tea; would you like some?" you'll encourage your guests to enjoy your hospitality. Similarly, at snack time, refrain from asking if anybody would like anything to eat. Just put the food out and offer it. Then everybody will freely decide whether to have some.

Your guests shouldn't feel that they must earn your hospitality. Don't show a guest who is a physician your skin rash or ask a lawyer how you can incorporate your business. If you need to tap their professional expertise, call them the next day at the office. Asking one of your guests to perform is not a good idea, unless you know that he or she would like to (and that your other guests would enjoy the performance). Your dinner guests are under no obligation to help you in the kitchen either before or after the meal. If they offer to and you are comfortable with it, accept with a simple thank-you.

The rules change for houseguests who stay a week or more. Then you can certainly expect some help from them. In a graceful book celebrating the graceful life, Dwight Currie tells an amusing story of hospitality:

A few years ago I arrived at a friend's home at the onset of a weeklong visit. He greeted me at the door with a hearty, "Welcome! Make yourself at home!" I thanked him and assured him that I would indeed be comfortable. In response he elaborated, "My house is your house!" So again, I thanked him for his hospitality—and again he upped the ante. "My kitchen is your kitchen," he said, and before I could reply, his welcome continued: "My grocery store is your grocery store," he explained, "my stove is your stove, my dishwasher is your dishwasher, my broom is your broom." He stopped, grinned at me, and asked, "Do you get the idea?" I nodded.

Currie recalls how liberating it was for him as a houseguest to be told that he was expected to take care of himself and to do his share. He relaxed and really did feel at home. Now, Currie's friend's impish frankness may not be your style. The point is that if you let your houseguests help you with sundry light chores they won't feel that they are imposing on you and will enjoy your hospitality more.

Make sure your guests know that you are delighted to spend time with them, but take care not to overwhelm them with attention. Ask them if there is anything in particular that they would like to do. However, you may want to select a few possible activities before their arrival, thinking of the interests you have in common. As a considerate host you want them to realize that what you are planning is not just for their benefit but for your own as well. That art exhibit at the museum you have been meaning to see for the last several weeks? This is the perfect time to go: everybody wins. Alternate busy and quiet days. Overscheduling can be stressful and wearying for both hosts and guests.

Your guests should feel that although they are in someone else's home, they are still in charge of their time. About the art exhibit you might say: "We could go to the museum tomorrow, but if you'd like to be on your own, that's all right, too." In turn, feel free to claim time for yourself when you have commitments to tend to ("I hope you won't mind being on your own tomorrow afternoon. I have some things to do"). Sometimes you may need to be alone for a while as a break from your duties as a host—just to recharge. Make sure that your guests can reach you in case of an emergency, but make it clear to them that the time you claim as yours is really yours.

Finally, an essential goal of playing host is that of getting to know your guests better and strengthening your mutual bonds. To do that you only need to listen and talk from the heart.

20. Be a Considerate Guest

In the age of E-mail and the cellular telephone, there is no excuse
for arriving unannounced at a friend's home. When invited to a
dinner or a party, respect both times of arrival and of departure.
Don't overstay your welcome, but don't leave too soon. Rely on
common sense and on your hosts' cues.

The good guest never brings surprise guests. If the invitation
is for you and a friend or you and your spouse, that means just
the two of you, no matter how convenient it would be for you to
include your cousin and her husband visiting from Albany. Or
your children.

It is your hosts' prerogative to open the party to children. If
their invitation does not mention children, it's likely that they are
not included. Don't lobby for a special permission. If you do that,
you put undue pressure on your hosts. At that point they can say
a reluctant "yes," thus being unfair to all other guests who did
follow the rules (by either declining the invitation or enlisting

baby-sitters), or they can tell you no to your face. Either way, they are facing an unpleasant task. This is not what they should receive in return for the kind gesture of inviting you.

Never assume that Fido or Boots are welcome. One thought: allergies. Another: compatibility with resident animals. One more: the damage your animal can do to someone else's home. It is your responsibility to find a safe place for your companion animals while you enjoy someone's hospitality.

Never force an invitation. Somebody's suggestion such as "Maybe sometime you can join us on our boat" doesn't give you permission to immediately propose a sailing date. If you are invited to spend two weeks at your friends' house, remain for just two weeks. By doing so you will respect both your friends' space and their time. Let Jane Austen's witty observation be your guidance: "It was a delightful visit—perfect in being much too short." As a considerate houseguest you will assume that the premises are smoke-free, put luggage and clothes out of sight upon your arrival, and abstain from rearranging the furniture in your bedroom. Make your bed every morning, unless that's the task of the household help, in which case you will simply pull up sheet and blankets. If you are sharing a bathroom, don't linger in it. Whether you are sharing it or not, keep the bathroom clean and tidy.

Your guiding principle is that you want to leave somebody else's space as undisturbed as possible. You may turn the television on in your bedroom (keeping the volume low), but your hosts' records, tapes, and CDs are not to be touched. Rise and retire following the household's routine. Refrain from wandering around the house. Curiosity is not a good reason to appear uninvited in your hosts' bedrooms, study, basement, or attic. All these are off-limits spaces.

Use your portable telephone (in your room or any other place where you won't be a nuisance). Make sure that the peace of the house is not disturbed by your incoming calls. If you need to use the house telephones, ask permission to do so and charge your long-distance calls to your card. Your hosts should know what your plans for the day are. Leave a telephone number where they can reach you. If you tell them you'll return at seven, do so; if you find that you are going to be late, call. Don't bring unannounced visitors to the house.

Return promptly anything you borrowed. When you leave, don't take with you anything that doesn't belong to you. Even if your stay is not as pleasant as you expected, keep a pleasant disposition and show appreciation for your hosts' efforts to show you a good time. Thank them warmly before leaving and send them a thank-you note upon your return home. Never mention any inconvenience you might have experienced as their guest. When mentioning your stay to a third party, speak kindly of your hosts, focusing on the best experiences you had with them. Don't divulge anything that might embarrass them.

We are guests even when we stay at a hotel. In today's hotels only a thin, flimsy wall, often porous to sound, separates us from other guests. Be considerate. I remember waking up very early in the morning in a hotel room a few years ago. Virginia and I had no plans to leave the room in the next couple of hours. She reminded me of this as I was getting ready to take a shower. The night before, she had noticed that bathroom waterwork noises traveled almost unhampered from room to room. Why not wait an hour or so before starting all that racket? Our next-door neighbors would surely appreciate it. Good idea. I wished I had thought of it myself.

Be aware that your hotel room space is also the space of those who work there. Generous tipping doesn't give you a license to be insensitive and slovenly. Before leaving your room, make sure that all remnants of food are tucked away in the wastebaskets, that your underwear is not strewn on the floor, that the toilet has been flushed, and that the bathroom is not flooded. The cleaning crew, who have seen it all, will appreciate your thoughtfulness.

A NOTE ON NOT ABUSING THE THINGS OF OTHERS

I had been relaxing for about an hour in the rocking comfort of a brand-new, spotlessly clean coach of a New York–bound train. At a scheduled stop in Delaware, a young man and a young woman got on. Pulling two enormous pieces of luggage, they started to laboriously make their way down the aisle. They soon stopped. Without hesitation, the young man nimbly climbed on top of an aisle seat and, with the help of his companion, struggled to lift one of the unwieldy suitcases onto the overhead racks. Then the young woman climbed onto the next seat to complete the operation. And on they went stamping all over the brand-new seats—armrests included, for better reach—until the second suitcase was in place as well.

Perhaps we don't respect things because we have so many of them. In a very affluent society nothing seems to have real value—especially, of course, things that don't belong to us. Maybe I should have said something to my young fellow travelers, something along the lines of "Have you thought that if everybody stamped all over new seats, they wouldn't last very long, that the train company factors the costs of destroyed property into the price of its tickets, and that many passengers—I among them—prefer to travel on clean rather than dirty seats?"

I've been known to speak up on such occasions, but this time I was not up to a confrontation. *It will go in the book,* I thought, and here it is. Few things would gratify me as much as a rediscovered respect for things belonging to others. Not abusing the property of others (or of the community) is one of the ways in which we respect others. It is an essential part of being considerate guests, no matter where we are: in an airplane, in a friend's home, in a movie theater, in a doctor's office, in a public library, or in a public square.

21. Think Twice Before Asking for Favors

DON'T ASK FOR FAVORS TOO CASUALLY OR TOO OFTEN—
RECOGNIZE THE AMOUNT OF EFFORT YOU'RE REQUESTING. IF
POSSIBLE, ACCOMPLISH YOUR TASK IN SOME OTHER WAY. . . . BE
CLEARLY GRATEFUL FOR A FAVOR DONE. EVEN IF THE TASK
APPEARED EASY FOR THE PERSON, GIVE FULL CREDIT—THE PER-
SON MAY BE KEEPING THE DIFFICULTIES OR UNPLEASANTNESS
OF THE EFFORT FROM YOU.
—*Janet Gallant*

I have always felt ambivalent about favors. True, we use them to help one another every day of our lives. However, a request for a favor is often an imposition, it can also be a request for a privilege unfair to others, and, finally, when we receive a favor we are, to a lesser or greater extent, beholden to those who granted it. All this is reason enough to think twice before asking for favors. I don't mean that there should be no place for favors in our lives. What I do suggest is that we always consider trying first to be the solvers of our own problems. We are so used to relying on favors that we often forget to look for the alternative—and we also forget that doing the work ourselves in the long run is more gratifying and satisfying.

There are two kinds of favors. The first affects only those doing the asking and the granting of it. Virginia and I are reading in our lawn chairs. As she gets up and heads toward the kitchen, I ask her if she would please do me the favor of refilling my glass with iced tea. This is a very simple request. I am asking her to do something for me; she's kind enough to do it; only the two of us are affected by our exchange. She may perceive this as a small imposition, and I may feel I owe her a small debt of gratitude. But that's the extent of it.

Favors of the second kind have consequences affecting others as well. Virginia is now ready to drive to the library where she works. She almost makes it out the door when I stop her. Without really thinking, I ask her if she would please get for me the current issue of a journal I need for my work at home during the weekend. On the surface, this favor is similar to the one involving the glass of iced tea. However, both she and I know that the library's current issues of periodicals are not supposed to circulate. By keeping the journal at home for the weekend I will prevent others from having access to it. What I'm doing is asking her to break the rules of her workplace and potentially inconvenience her patrons for the sake of my convenience. Is it all right? Should she do me the favor? Of course not. Time for me to get in the car for a trip to the library.

There is nothing wrong with asking for favors of the first kind as long as we keep our requests reasonable. The system works until someone ends up doing most of the asking and someone else most of the granting. Fairness is of paramount importance here.

Fairness should also be at work in favor granting of the second kind. We should always consider that someone, somewhere, may pay the price for the favor we are granting or are granted, that our advantage may put someone else at a disadvantage.

A bad cold keeps Arnold's two young children from going to school. Arnold could hire a baby-sitter or take a day off from work to care for them. Instead, he asks his boss the favor of allowing him to bring them to work with him. Now we have two coughing, sneezing, bored, and cranky children interfering with the normal activities of Arnold's office. Arnold pays as much attention as he can to his work while he tries to keep his children under control and entertained. Finally he gives up, rounds the children up, and goes home early.

Now, remember that Arnold had at least two alternatives that entailed no imposition or disruption. He chose the easy way out (not so easy, actually, in retrospect) rather than acting in a considerate and professional fashion. He put his boss on the spot by asking for a favor, he could not work effectively, and he unfairly burdened his coworkers with a problem that was, and should have remained, only his. The arrangement was also unfair to his children, who certainly deserved better care.

Refraining from asking for favors is difficult but perhaps not as difficult as saying, "No, thank you," to favors offered. Suppose that Arnold had called his office to say he had a problem with his children and his boss's reply was, "Why don't you bring them to work?" And suppose that Arnold had replied, "It's very kind of you to offer, but I wouldn't be comfortable with it. I'm going to find another solution. I may just be half an hour late." That would have been a rather impressive way of managing the small crisis.

But what about friends? Aren't favors what friends are for? If you are my friend, shouldn't I expect a treatment of privilege from you? Isn't that, after all, the way you show that you are my friend? I must say that I never thought of friendship in these terms. To me, friendship is about how one feels with friends, not about what one can get from them. The occasional exchange of favors will occur in any friendship, but no real friendship is based on the expectation that our friends will be providers of favors. What kind of friend would you rather you be? The kind who asks for favors in the name of friendship or the kind who is careful to ask for as few favors as possible out of respect for his or her friends?

The principle that first you try to solve your problems on your own and only turn to others as a last resort applies to friends. We have an obligation to show our friends that we are turning to them for a favor not because it happens to be convenient for us to do so but because of a compelling reason. Furthermore, no reason is compelling enough to make us ask our friends to grant us a favor we would be unwilling to grant them if the need arose.

Our basic beliefs are not suspended when it comes to dealing with friends. If you believe in honesty, you bring it into your friendship rather than making it a casualty of friendship. Should friends expect that you will recommend them for a job for which they clearly are not qualified? Or, to put it bluntly, are friends expected to lie for friends? No, friends are not expected to lie for friends, and friends don't ask friends to lie for them. When you ask your friend to do something unethical or illegal in the name of your friendship you have already ceased to be a friend.

WHAT TO THINK WHEN YOU'RE THINKING TWICE

- Do I *need* to ask for this favor or am I just looking for an easy solution to my problem?

- Is what I'm asking ethical and legal?

- Is it fair and reasonable to ask this of this person? Would *I* be comfortable granting this favor?

- Who else, other than me, is this going to affect? Is the granting of this favor going to put others at a disadvantage or hurt them?

- Will I be comfortable being beholden to this person? (It's a good idea to refrain from asking a favor of someone who doesn't have your full trust and respect.)

- If I am granted the favor, how is this going to affect my relationship with this person? And if I am denied the favor?

Regarding this last point, think of the conflicting feelings stirred in friends who have turned to one another for the lending and borrowing of money. A friendship can be strengthened by the exchange of such a favor, but it can also be wounded beyond recovery.

22. Refrain from Idle Complaints

DON'T CURSE THE DARKNESS — LIGHT A CANDLE.

—Chinese proverb

THEN I DO NOT THINK OF ALL THE MISERY, BUT OF THE GLORY
THAT REMAINS. *—Anne Frank*

This rule is not about justified remonstrations. A civil voicing of
your displeasure is certainly appropriate when you must deal with
the morose and/or incompetent salesclerk, the truant waiter, the
hostile cabdriver, the disruptive child, the pushy coworker, the
unreasonable boss, the arrogant law enforcer, the nosy in-law, and
the noisy neighbor—to name just a few. In these cases you speak
your mind not only out of self-respect and to do something about
your current problem but also in the hope of helping those who
will have to deal with the problem maker in the future. There is
always a chance that your speaking up will cause good change.

This rule is not about the occasional therapeutic sharing of woes,
either. Indeed, there can be comfort in complaining. What concerns me here, instead, is the continuous or recurring complaining
that is an unwarranted spreading of misery. It is the kind that
bespeaks helplessness rather than assertiveness, is more interested
in assigning blame than in finding solutions, and is rooted in the

feeling that life is unfair. Now, disappointments, disheartening setbacks, and dreams that fail to become reality are an inevitable part of being alive. Every day you spend on earth, however, also gives you an abundance of reasons to be grateful. It is up to you to choose between giving in to dissatisfaction and resentment and embracing contentment and joy. My suggestion is that you make every effort to start walking toward joy today, not only for your own good but for the good of those closest to you as well.

What's wrong, exactly, with idle complaining? It is bad because concentrating on problems rather than solutions reinforces a pessimistic outlook on life. And it is bad for those around you because it spreads your pessimism to them. Pessimism is like deliberate trudging in the mud. When you complain, you stick your unfortunate listeners in your own mud and you drag them along with you for no good reason. When you are about to yield to the temptation of going on a tirade about what's wrong with your life or the world, just stop and think. Right now you are underestimating your power to influence your life—and that of others—for the better. Right now you have the choice to redirect your energies away from a futile exercise in negativism. Yes, there are a thousand ways in which things could be better, but there is also plenty that you can do about that. Tranquillity, joy, and happiness are, to a large extent, gifts we give to ourselves. They are the result of our smart choices in the way we think and the way we act. There is no way to erase misery from the face of the earth, but you can always focus on the glory that remains. Begin by letting go of unproductive complaining.

Identify, first by yourself and then with the help of someone who knows you well, recurring themes of complaint. What are they? Not receiving enough recognition at work? Not making enough money? The growing burden of taxes? The hardships of commuting? That stubbornly uncooperative weather? The deterioration of retail service? The crisis in education? The self-centeredness of the young? The aches and pains of middle age? Your insufficient medical coverage? Never having enough time for yourself? After you've made a list of recurring themes, choose one and expunge it from your repertoire as your project of the month. Monitor yourself for the entire month. Whenever you feel the urge to complain about the theme for the month make sure you stop. Don't just try to forget about it, though. Instead, refocus on problem solving. What are the reasons for the problem? What can *you* do about it? The following month you will get rid of another theme of complaint, and on you'll go, until you have checked off all the items on your list.

Complaining can be an exercise in self-obfuscation. When we complain, we often project onto others our dissatisfaction with how we are handling our own lives. By complaining about what others do to us, we avoid recognizing our own weaknesses and mistakes and thus miss the chance to bring positive change into our lives. Behind a complaint about service quality in a restaurant, for example, may lurk the frustration at our inability to stay on a strict diet. Someone's sharp criticism of his or her small child's teacher may spring from misgivings about leaving the child in a stranger's care for a large part of the day. We complain about the world because we are unhappy about ourselves. Maintaining awareness of this simple psychological shifting mechanism will make it easier for you to bring your complaining under control.

"I beseech you by all angels," wrote Ralph Waldo Emerson, "to hold your peace, and not pollute the morning, to which all the housemates bring serene and pleasant thoughts, by corruption and groans." Emerson's words keep coming back to me. Indeed, I believe that it is a very good thing to refrain from polluting others' serene morning with our discontent. Should their morning be less than serene already, you wouldn't want to add to their own reasons for discontent. Encourage them instead to look hard for reasons to cheer up. Look hard along with them. Few will ever fault you for being a relentless spotter of silver linings.

SERVICE EXCELLENCE AND THE CIVIL WORKPLACE

I value good service. I appreciate a salesperson who is prompt, attentive, courteous, and professional. I am willing to reward good service, but I will, on occasion, make my displeasure known when I believe the quality of service is particularly bad. I do not think that the customer is always right. The customer is right when he or she is polite and his or her demands are reasonable. A reciprocal showing of respect should be part of any transaction between customer and service provider. By the way, when it comes to bad service a large number of complaints is not always the worst of signs. Sometimes it is a decrease or the absence of complaints that is ominous. This may mean that people are not reporting their dissatisfaction and giving up on seeking redress.

What goes into making a good service provider? Good interpersonal skills, a strong work ethic, and careful training. To these I would add: a civil workplace. When we think of service we think mostly of the relationship between employee and customer. Service is what the provider does for the customer; it is about improving the customer's experience. But the employee's experience has a bearing on the customer's. The quality of service is related to the quality of life of those who provide the service. A stressed, overburdened, fatigued, harassed, or underpaid employee is not likely to provide the best service. A civil workplace is a serene workplace and a productive one. It is productive in more ways than one, and one of the things it produces is good service.

If the employees are full of energy and patience because their workload is reasonable, if they are at ease because they are asked to do things within their job specifications, if they work in harmony because they do not feel threatened or defensive, then all this has a positive effect on the customer's experience. Encouraging civility in the workplace is becoming a corporate goal in our diverse, hurried, stressed, and litigation-prone society. A civil workplace is good for the workers, since the workers' quality of life is improved in such an environment. But a civil workplace is also good for the customers, since the quality of the service they receive from happier and more relaxed service providers is improved.

Employees should expect to work in a civil workplace. Such a workplace is, however, a goal achieved and maintained through every employee's effort. Corporate responsibility does not erase individual responsibility. We don't wait for civility to happen. We work for it when we are smart enough to imagine its rewards.

23. Accept and Give
Constructive Criticism

A GOOD FRIEND WILL LISTEN TO US WITHOUT JUDGMENT, AC-
CEPT THE INTENSITY OF OUR FEELINGS, RESPECT OUR PAIN, AND
EXPRESS CONCERN. A REALLY GOOD FRIEND WILL, IN ADDITION,
HELP US TO SEE OUR SITUATION IN A NEW WAY.
—Mark I. Rosen

OUR CRITICS ARE THE UNPAID GUARDIANS OF OUR SOULS.
—Corrie ten Boom

I HATE JUDGMENTS THAT ONLY CRUSH AND DON'T TRANSFORM.
—Elias Canetti

I try to give constructive criticism whenever circumstances suggest that it's the right thing to do. I must confess that I really
enjoy giving it. (If I didn't, I doubt if I would have found my
past twenty-five years as a teacher as gratifying as I have.) But I
also enjoy being at the receiving end of criticism. This is a welcome opportunity to learn—mostly about myself but also about
my critics and about life. Although criticism is not always directed
at us with the noblest of intentions, nothing prevents us from
looking at it as a gift to be put to good use.

To criticize is a serious business and sometimes an awesome
responsibility. Before you speak make sure that your intention is

to help with a problem and not to humiliate, manipulate, or exact revenge. Are you sure there *is* a problem and that you have a sound sense of *what* it is? Is this the right moment to address it? Are you so upset that it's probably a good idea to wait? What is the emotional state of the other person? Are there other people around who shouldn't be privy to the exchange? Finally, consider asking the other person's permission to broach the delicate subject: "I've been wondering about something you did. Would you mind if I shared my thoughts with you?" Of course, in the presence of imminent danger you'll speak without hesitation. A typical case in point is that of the partying driver who needs to be told that he or she is drinking too much. You want to act immediately not only for the driver's sake but also on behalf of those who might end up being hurt by his or her behavior.

> BEING TO ADVISE OR REPREHEND ANY ONE, CONSIDER WHETHER IT OUGHT TO BE IN PUBLICK OR IN PRIVATE; PRESENTLY OR AT SOME OTHER TIME, IN WHAT TERMS TO DO IT & IN REPROVING SHEW NO SIGN OF CHOLAR, BUT DO IT WITH ALL SWEETNESS AND MILDNESS.
>
> —*George Washington*

To make your criticism constructive and effective:

- Identify an issue, rather than launching an attack on the person. Point to a specific incident. Say: "I think the way you defended our team's work yesterday may not have been the most effective." Don't say: "You're just hopeless." Consider prefacing your critical remarks with positive ones: it may make your interlocutor more receptive. As you bring forward his or her good qualities and things he or she did right, be careful not to sound patronizing.

- Describe what you have observed rather than uttering accusations or engaging in name-calling. Say: "There seemed to be an expectation in the room of more precise data on projected sales." Don't say: "That was just stupid, going in unprepared like that."

- Show that you understand how the other person may feel: "The same thing has happened to me more than once. When you know that your product is good, it seems that everyone else should be smart enough to know it, too." Don't forget, however, that your focus here is not on past similar situations but on the present and the future. Don't stray from the problem at hand.

- Suggest a solution if you feel this is the right time to do so. You may also volunteer to work toward finding one: "If you want, we can look together for ways to present our side of the story again."

- Remain calm, kind, and empathic throughout the exchange. End on a positive note: "This is not the end of the world, just something to take care of."

RECEIVING CRITICISM

When we reject outright the criticism that comes our way we forgo a precious source of knowledge and wisdom. I don't mean to say that all criticism is good. But in most criticism there is something good enough to take to heart. It is unfortunate that we often consider ourselves the only legitimate judges of our actions. A good, realistic sense of self-worth must leave room for the kind of improvement that only criticism and advice can produce.

> LET ME NEVER FALL INTO THE VULGAR MISTAKE OF DREAM-
> ING THAT I AM PERSECUTED WHENEVER I AM CONTRA-
> DICTED.   —*Ralph Waldo Emerson*

Rather than thinking of your critic as the enemy, try to be as open-minded as possible. If you are not too busy building your defenses, you will be able at least to listen. This is the first important step in receiving criticism. Listen as though your critic were not speaking about you but rather about someone else. Ask yourself: *Is this criticism valid?* Should it happen to ring true to you, go ahead and simply agree with it. Don't waste precious energy and time (both your critic's and yours) denying the charges, painstakingly qualifying your agreement, or questioning your critic's motives. Just say a plain and honest "I believe you're right" and start thinking about the changes you want to make. If you are not ready to do that, it's perfectly all right to postpone your final response: "This is certainly food for thought. Thank you for your honest opinion. I will need some time to think about it." Should the criticism appear totally unwarranted, say so with tranquil firmness: "I'm afraid I can't agree with that," "I don't recognize myself in your characterization," "I know that's not what I meant." Don't make your response a counterattack. Be assertive, not abusive, even if you believe that your critic is being unfair or utterly hostile.

Criticism doesn't have to be offered with friendly intentions to be useful. It is up to you to make it so. Many years ago my good grades in school became the talk of my little world of family and friends. Although I was embarrassed by the attention and praise, I was also pleased. One day one of my friends remarked unkindly that he was sick and tired of all the fuss everybody was making about my grades. It was clear to me that I was included in the "everybody" he was targeting with his criticism. I knew immediately that his outburst had some merit. The whole thing was indeed becoming tiresome. Although I didn't know what I could have done differently to avoid getting to that point, I knew that there was a lesson in the incident. Something good (my success in school, in this case) can easily become a liability if it's not managed wisely. It's not only adversity that requires able steering but the good times as well. The simple and yet invaluable insight I gained thanks to my friend's criticism still shapes my actions, after all these years.

It's almost impossible not to enjoy the sense of validation that comes with praise, but it is criticism that makes us learn what we are unable or unwilling to learn by ourselves. Whenever we turn our back on good criticism we do so at our own peril.

24. Respect the Environment and Be Gentle to Animals

WE NEED TO ESTABLISH, AS BASIC GOALS FOR OUR SOCIETY, BOTH PRESERVING THE ENVIRONMENT'S HEALTH AND INCORPORATING THE ROUTINE EXPERIENCE OF NATURE INTO OUR EVERYDAY LIVES.   —*Stephen R. Kellert*

MORE THAN EVER, PEOPLE VIEW THEIR DOGS AS FAMILY, WITH ALL THE RIGHTS OF THE DOMINANT SPECIES WITHOUT TAILS.
                                    —*Timothy Egan*

THE ENVIRONMENT

Many Americans believe that incivility is a serious problem, that the problem has been getting worse in recent years, and that the situation is not likely to change for the better anytime soon. Is the perception of a decline in civic virtues and social graces in America borne out by reality? It depends on what we choose to measure. When we speak of a decline in civility, we usually refer to a crisis regarding established forms of concern, respect, and deference. As we do so, we tend to ignore new forms that take the place of old ones. Maybe the number of youngsters holding onto their bus seats while pregnant women and elderly gentlemen are precariously swaying in the aisle is on the rise. But then so, I believe, is the number of those who treat members of racial minorities with genuine respect. I am not saying that the advances in new civility should make us forget what we are losing. Many of us care about the established endangered forms to the extent that we perceive their decline as a threat to the quality of our lives. What I am suggesting is that we don't forget that the decline is not cutting across-the-board. It may be hard to believe, but in certain areas of our everyday behavior we are becoming more civil rather than less. A shining example of new civility is the remarkably serious commitment to the cause of the environment on the part of an extraordinary number of people from all walks of life. (More on all this in part 3.)

An age-old component of humanity's relationship with nature is fear: nature is dangerous, so we must defend ourselves from it. Over the past several decades, this traditional attitude has been eclipsed, at least partially, by one of concern. The new attitude is: nature is in danger, so we must defend it from ourselves. It is not that we have lost the ability to regard nature with awe and fear. Flash floods, brush fires, earthquakes, and hurricanes are powerful reminders of its might. But we feel much more in control, or able to cope, than we ever did in the past. And we think that we are much more of a threat to nature than nature is to us. Only two or three generations ago it was commonplace to describe progress as the subjugation of nature by man. Today we are more likely to think of progress as freeing nature from the lethal embrace of a recklessly wasteful and polluting humanity.

WE DO NOT INHERIT THE EARTH FROM OUR ANCESTORS, WE BORROW IT FROM OUR CHILDREN. —*Native American saying*

The last thirty years of the twentieth century saw the preservation of the environment become, as Amitai Etzioni says, a "shared core value" in Western societies and in a number of non-Western ones as well. Protecting the environment has been called a new commandment. Throwing an empty plastic bottle into a river today is viewed as a threat to the health of the planet. Millions of people all around the world perform daily innumerable acts of regard toward the environment that would have been inconceivable only one or two generations ago.

In the wake of the ecological revolution, it's impossible to be civil without an active concern for the health of our badly wounded planet. What this means varies from person to person. For some, the protection of the environment is a primary personal goal to be pursued relentlessly. For many, it is simply a serious concern. Here is a minimal list of responsibilities for the ecologically minded:

- Don't litter.

- Don't use products that have been proven harmful to the environment.

- Take the time to recycle. Limit your use of unrecyclable products. Dispose of anything potentially polluting in a safe, ecologically sound way.

- Purchase products made with recycled materials.

- Conserve water. Run washers only when you have a full load. Make sure your flushing tanks are not wasteful.

- Conserve electricity. Turn off lights when you don't need them. Turn down your furnace and air conditioner when you are not at home.

- Conserve fuel. Think of fuel efficiency when purchasing a car. Make one car trip rather than many to run errands.

Walk or ride a bicycle whenever you can and it is safe to
do so.

• Use alternative sources of energy.

THE ANIMALS

> THE QUESTION IS NOT, CAN THEY *REASON*? NOR, CAN THEY
> *TALK*? BUT, CAN THEY *SUFFER*?   —*Jeremy Bentham*

Are we kinder to animals than the generations that came before
us? I believe we are. We seem to be growing less tolerant of the
mistreatment of animals. That animals have rights is today a well-
entrenched notion in the conscience of millions. Even the notion
that humans shouldn't claim superiority over other species is making inroads. Cruelty against animals is a crime in every state of
the Union. Hundreds of thousands of people are involved in or-
ganized pro-animal activities. Organizations such as the Humane
Society of the United States, the Animal Legal Defense Fund, the
Best Friends Animal Sanctuary, the American Society for the Pre-
vention of Cruelty to Animals, and People for the Ethical Treatment of Animals may differ in goals, policies, and strategies, but
they are all part of a mighty network of animal advocacy that has
no precedent in human history. Many Americans think of their
companion animals as members of their family. You may remember the national outcry of indignation that followed the death of
Leo, the little dog an enraged motorist threw into oncoming traffic
in San Jose, California. A few weeks after the dreadful incident the
reward for the perpetrator's capture was in the tens of thousands
of dollars.

As the son of a veterinarian, I remember many a childhood

afternoon spent with my father in the soothing company of pigs, cows, and chickens. I remember caressing little calves on their coarse black-and-white foreheads as one of my first thrills. As I grew in age, my ability to see any encounter with an animal as a gift also grew. Animals now have the power to reconcile me with life. They are for me an endless source of wonder, serenity, and charm. And, just as it is for me, their companionable, healing presence is a priceless blessing for millions of other people. As decent human beings, we can reciprocate by taking responsible and gentle care of animals.

- Never neglect animals. Never use brutal force against them. Treat them with both respect and affection.

- If you are not prepared to care for an animal 365 days a year, don't get one. If you can make this commitment, consider adopting from the local animal shelter. Millions of healthy, unwanted cats and dogs are put to sleep in shelters every year. Many animal lovers are fervent advocates of the spaying and neutering of family animals.

- Puppies and kittens that seemed such a fine gift idea at Christmas can become unwanted burdens by summer. Don't give or accept animals as gifts unthinkingly.

- Abandoning a family animal is never an option.

- Keep your animals safe. Keep them away from toxic chemicals and plants. If you must leave your animals in your car unattended, make sure it's only for a few minutes. Don't forget to leave a window partially open. Don't leave animals in your car if the temperature outside is above 75 degrees.

- Be kind not only to your animals but to those of others as well. If your dog is nervous in the presence of other pets, keep him on a short leash and warn other pet owners. Make sure your dog is wearing a muzzle not just if the law requires it but also if you believe it's the safe thing to do.

Among the civilizing lessons we want to impress upon the next generation is that the way we treat animals is a measure of our character.

25. Don't Shift Responsibility and Blame

We are all familiar with the drill: Somebody at fault will try to minimize his or her responsibility by blaming someone else— quite often the wronged party. Thus the main characteristics of this exercise in rudeness are obfuscation and unfairness. Following are four vignettes showcasing instances of this very common rude behavior and their civil alternatives.

CUSTOMER: "I'd like to ship these books book-rate and airmail."

EMPLOYEE: "Airmail? I never do that."

CUSTOMER: "Do you mean that there is no book-rate airmail service or that this is not the right window?"

EMPLOYEE: "No, I just never do that. I always do surface mail with books."

CUSTOMER: "But book-rate airmail service does exist, right?"

EMPLOYEE: "Nobody does it. I don't know what the rate is."

CUSTOMER: "Would you mind checking?"

EMPLOYEE: "If you want me to. I never do that."

At this point Employee lets out a big sigh, reluctantly climbs down from his stool, and walks to the next window to consult with a coworker. Customer wonders for a moment if she was in any way at fault, only to realize that she wasn't. Book-rate airmail *is* one of the services the post office provides. It's Employee who unprofessionally made her feel as though there was something wrong with her request. As she waits for him to come back, she daydreams of a civil version of the exchange:

CUSTOMER: "I'd like to ship these books book-rate and airmail."

EMPLOYEE: "I'm sorry, ma'am; I'm not familiar with the rates. It'll take me just a minute to find out what they are."

End of exchange.

————

RECENT BRIDE (on the telephone): "I just received a separate bill of seventy-five dollars from you for a bride's bouquet. But the bouquet was also itemized with all the other flowers in the general bill, which I already paid."

FLORIST: "It was a one-hundred-dollar arrange-
                    ment that I gave you for seventy-five
                    dollars, remember? It was a very special
                    price. Because of that somebody didn't
                    realize it was already on the other bill."

RECENT BRIDE: "But it *was* on the other bill, which I
                    paid. So we're even, right?"

FLORIST: "Yes, I just wanted to explain how you
                    got that invoice. It was because of the
                    special price. We never charge so little
                    for that kind of bouquet."

Recent Bride *was* double-billed for her bouquet. This is the
essential fact in the exchange. Florist is at fault, but you could
hardly tell by the spin he gives to the incident. He switches Recent
Bride's attention to the discount. Both in his words and his tone
the implication is: *You are not very grateful for the special treatment
you received.* Recent Bride knows she is right, and is offended by
Florist's obfuscation. She knows very well the simple answer she
was entitled to:

"The second bill was sent in error. I apologize."

———

GROCERY SHOPPER #1:   "Ma'am, you didn't have to
                      push me. You could have just
                      told me I was in your way by
                      the produce scale and I would
                      have stepped aside."

GROCERY SHOPPER #2:   "I didn't see you."

GROCERY SHOPPER #1: "You didn't see me and yet you shoved me aside?"

GROCERY SHOPPER #2: "Boy, somebody got up on the wrong side of the bed this morning!"

What happens here? Grocery Shopper #2 refuses to accept responsibility for her rude treatment of Grocery Shopper #1. When Grocery Shopper #1 challenges her flimsy excuse, she turns the tables on him by faulting him for being cranky. Her shoving, the uncivil act with which the incident originated, gets lost behind her defensive smoke screen. Grocery Shopper #1 never gets to hear the simple, decent words that soothe the bruised soul:

"I'm sorry."

———

HOST: "I'm calling to let you know that we have switched our dinner to Tuesday. So, we'll see you and Sayeed around five P.M. on Tuesday instead of Wednesday, OK?"

GUEST: "I'm sorry, but we have other plans for Tuesday. Wednesday was fine, but Tuesday is really a problem for us."

HOST: "Oh, it's only a twenty-four-hour difference. I'm sure you can do something."

GUEST: "I'm sorry, but on such short notice there isn't much we can do."

HOST: "We have talked to everybody. Everybody else will be there."

GUEST: "Thank you for your invitation, but we just can't."

HOST: "But we have so much food. Everything is ready. You *must* come. What is it that you have to do?"

Host is the one with the problem. He changed the date of his dinner. However, he tries to manipulate Guest into feeling that he, Guest, is somehow at fault. All of a sudden Guest is the problem maker. Why is Guest making such a big deal of such a little thing? Nobody else seemed to mind the change of date. And think of all that good food that will be wasted. Host's final salvo is asking outright what prevents Guest from going. There is a touch of exasperation there. Of course, there can't possibly be anything compelling enough to prevent Guest from attending Host's all-important dinner!

Here is the civil version of the same dialogue, one in which Host civilly abstains from playing the manipulation game:

HOST: "I'm calling to let you know that we had to change the date of the dinner at our home to Tuesday. I apologize for the short notice. You don't think that you and Sayeed can still make it, by any chance? We would be so glad to have you."

GUEST: "I'm sorry, but we have other plans for Tuesday. Wednesday was fine, but Tuesday is really a problem for us."

HOST: "I'm really sorry, too, but I understand. We'll try to do better the next time."

"FOR TO BE RUDE TO HIM WAS COURTESY"

It's a question I've heard many times since I started giving talks on civility and manners: "Are we always to be polite or are there circumstances that call for a less than civil response?" When I hear this question or one of its variations, such as "If someone is rude to us, can we be rude in return?" I am reminded of a famous line in Dante's *Divine Comedy*. The line, from canto 33 of the *Inferno,* reads *"e cortesia fu lui esser villano,"* which John Ciardi translates as "for to be rude to him was courtesy." Dante is referring there to his own treatment of Friar Alberigo, a notorious traitor whom he encounters on the frozen lake of Cocytus. Given the circumstances, Dante argues—dealing with a rogue enduring eternal punishment at the bottom of Hell—I was right in being discourteous to him; caddishness was the correct choice.

With all due understanding for Father Dante's behavior in the netherworld, I simply cannot conceive of any circumstance in our own daily lives when it would be appropriate or advantageous to be rude or boorish. The powerful combination of self-respect and respect for others should make it almost impossible for us to choose incivility, if we manage to remain clearheaded even in challenging situations.

But what if we are dealing with somebody whom we don't respect or who says or does something we believe to be wrong? The answer is simple: let's not lose sight of our own standards of behavior, of our own rules of engagement. It is possible to be civil and true to one's beliefs at the same time. The issue is not whether to stand firm or compromise but how to express our firmness. When we express it with poise rather than rudeness, not only are we truer to our better selves, but we infuse our dissent with a power that it wouldn't have otherwise. To brawl is human. To be civil works.

PART THREE

Culture Shock

Los Angeles, 1978. The young nurse glanced at her clipboard, then smiled at me and said: "Pier, the doctor will see you now." Astonished, I followed her into the examination room. Was she being utterly rude or did strangers routinely address one another by their first names in America? I must have been sixteen years old the last time I had been addressed informally by someone I saw for the first time in my life. Soon I would learn enough about American customs to know that the nurse had not been rude at all. She had used a code of informality that, no matter how much it surprised me, had been deemed appropriate for quite some time on this side of the Atlantic—and, in particular, on the West Coast.

People from other parts of the world are often taken aback by the prevalence of informality and familiarity in American social interaction. Things are changing in Europe, but formality of address is still widespread, especially among the older generation. It took my father fifteen years to start addressing his brother-in-law (someone with whom he had a friendly relationship) with the familiar pronoun *tu* instead of the formal *Lei*. Coming from this background, only after several years in this country was I able to see both the reasons for and the merits of American informality—and I am untiring now in telling my European friends not to mistake it for incivility. I still tend to err on the side of reserve (for example, unlike most of my colleagues, I address students at the university by their last name preceded by "Mr." or "Miss"). But I am often perfectly comfortable complying with a new acquaintance's request that I use his or her first name. And yes, I have also been known, on occasion, to be the first to make such a request.

However, there are some casual forms of address that are inappropriate between strangers. "Hiya guy" said on the phone by the cable company employee, having ascertained that he was indeed speaking with P. M. Forni. "What do you mean, 'hiya guy'?" I couldn't help replying. This elicited in turn—much to my pleased surprise—a scrambling "Good morning, sir."

Striking Through the Form
to the Substance

An unflagging belief in the absolute value of freedom, a strong egalitarian sentiment, and individualism are at the core of the American soul. These national peculiarities, which Alexis de Tocqueville memorably investigated, have long shaped Americans' attitudes toward good manners and civility:

> To evade the bondage of system and habit, of family maxims, class opinions, and, in some degree, of national prejudices; to accept tradition only as a means of information, and existing facts only as a lesson to be used in doing otherwise and doing better; to seek the reason of things for oneself, and in oneself alone; to tend to results without to be bound to means, and *to strike through the form to the substance*—such are the principal characteristics of what I shall call the philosophical method of the Americans. [My italics]

Of particular interest for our purposes is de Tocqueville's comment on form, a notion to which he returns in his chapter on the Americans' philosophical method: "[Americans] like to discern the object which engages their attention with extreme clearness; . . . they rid themselves of whatever separates them from it. . . . *This disposition of mind soon leads them to condemn forms, which they regard as useless and inconvenient veils placed between them and the truth*" (my italics).

Indeed, to this day we perceive as an American trait the predilection of substance over form, the daily and ubiquitous aberrations of spin doctors notwithstanding. We also consider American a pragmatic and straightforward approach in all things. Perhaps in America more than elsewhere manners, politeness, and civility— all having to do with form and formality—are called into question as veils hiding the bright face of truth. They are also suspect as markers of class privilege, as threats to freedom of self-expression, and as relics tainted by convention. Since change is good, says conventional wisdom, then following conventional rules can't be good. Therefore, civility must be bad. Besides, if we are meant to be the forgers of our own individual destinies, what is the use of anything having to do with convention?

I Did It My Way

Living among others, we must postpone or renounce the gratification of our desires. Having to follow written or unwritten rules that restrict our actions is an inevitable part of life. From this restriction the fantasy of freedom from the norm is born. From this our eager identification with the cinematic rule-breaking hero develops.

We glamorize the nonconformist and romanticize the maverick. "I did it my way," sings Frank Sinatra, and the applause is universal. Our culture seems particularly inclined to extol going against prevailing currents. "Make your own rules," we are told by innumerable glossy magazine and television commercials that present the preference for a brand of sports gear or a sports car as an act of healthful rebellion. But contrary to what happens in the world of fantasy, the breaking of rules in real life has real consequences for real people, as we have seen happen in too many American schools devastated by explosions of teen violence.

I am not arguing that unconventional behavior is always destructive or wrong. Departing from the norm can be not only acceptable but even necessary. Sometimes justice and self-respect conflict with established laws and conventions. Then we strive to establish new norms. But everyday life is made more pleasant, saner, and more healthful by the practice of the rules of civility that have withstood the test of time.

Authority on the Wane

❧❧

Why are we rude? The erosion of the principle of authority seems to have accelerated in the past several decades.

> FOR IT IS MY CONTENTION THAT WE ARE TEMPTED AND ENTITLED TO RAISE THIS QUESTION [WHAT WAS AUTHOR-ITY?] BECAUSE AUTHORITY HAS VANISHED FROM THE MODERN WORLD. —*Hannah Arendt*

The still-large capital of trust in their leaders that Americans held in the 1950s and early '60s has largely evaporated. Vietnam, Watergate, the Clinton scandals and sundry other scandals at both the national and local level have been substantial factors in the increase in distrust of and even disdain for the ruling class. Flawed politicians give politics a bad name and thus diminish authority itself.

The current crisis of authority is also a result of increased cultural literacy. When we nourish and refine our intellect, we often become more discerning and more critical. Mass education has swelled enormously the ranks of those unwilling to show unquestioning deference not only to established power but also to established values in general.

In recent decades we have seen all figures of authority lose authority, from politician to teacher to parent. The weakened authority of those who are entrusted with the task of promoting prosocial behaviors and preserving established values makes their message less credible and less likely to gain widespread acceptance. We can certainly connect the crisis of civility to a crisis of the very notion of authority.

We still live in the wake of the youth insurgency of the 1960s and '70s. Our culture is still shaped by the Counterculture, a momentous movement that invoked both deliverance from tradition and the embracing of authenticity. Many who grew up in those years have maintained an aversion to traditional rules of social conduct, which they see as hypocritical and repressive—another unfortunate by-product of bourgeois mentality and power. Their aversion has had a significant effect upon their children. The old ethic of self-discipline has given way to a new ethic of self-esteem and self-expression. This has endangered the practice of traditional civility.

A lot of good came from the questioning of dominant values in the confused and idealistic times of the youth revolution. We needed more self-esteem, and we needed more self-expression. We needed to look at power and politics with a more critical eye. And we needed to devote more political energy to the cause of those left at the margins of society, barely touched by prosperity, and with little hope of bettering their lot. But in the last forty years, as we were making strides toward a more just society, we were also becoming more and more self-absorbed.

The Age of the Self

We now live in an age of idolatry of the Self. We have persuaded ourselves that first and foremost we live to realize our own Selves for our own good. Having made the Self the central concern and value in our lives, we should not be surprised if self-centered behaviors have become more prevalent than altruistic ones. We shouldn't be surprised if civility has suffered. The more we focus on our Selves and our self-gratification, the less moral energy we have available to spend on others and the less attuned we are to others' well-being. We emerged from the upheaval of the 1960s and '70s with a stronger belief in the decency of equality and the goodness of freedom. What many of us are are learning or relearning now is the essential role that self-control plays in the lives of democracies. The emphasis on individual rights and entitlements in advanced democracies makes self-control particularly relevant to us. It is in part to prevent the massive intervention of government and the law in our everyday lives that we are expected to develop a civil discipline. As a system of self-regulation, civility assures the survival of self-determination. It is nothing less than the life-blood of democracies.

Living Among Strangers

Again, why are we rude? Anonymity is our constant companion. Many of our everyday encounters are with people we don't know. We are among strangers when we pump gas into our cars and when we pace a subway platform; when we wait at a traffic light and when we stand in line to renew our driver's licenses; when we ride the elevator at work and when we buy milk at the convenience store around the corner. We often have few significant ties with the communities in which we live. When this is the case, few also are our incentives to behave in a restrained, civil way. Gone are the days when merely knowing and being known by our next-door neighbors kept us in line. Living among strangers, we know that our crudeness or boorishness will go unreported—that we can get away with it. Nowhere in sight are the penalties of shame that would be paid in a more cohesive community.

Cut off by motorist A, motorist B reacts with a rude gesture. Determined not to lose face, motorist A responds in kind. In a frustrated and threatening dissonance of horn blowing, as tension turns to outrage, the two jostle their way to a final confrontation that might include a car crash, a fistfight, a shooting, or all of the above. Let us now suppose that just as this sequence of events is under way, just after the first show of finger puppetry, the two drivers realize that they know one another. Unless they are sworn enemies, the configuration of the incident is likely to change. Touched by embarrassment, they will immediately calm down as they pursue the new common goal of making light of what happened. They will smile, wave, vie in yielding the right-of-way, perhaps with a flourish of the hand reminiscent of courtly formality. What allowed for the defusing of the explosive situation? One essential element of volatility was eliminated. All of a sudden the rival was not an anonymous entity, a driving cipher, but a known individual. The elimination of anonymity was sufficient to reestablish the rules of civil social exchange and to secure a benign resolution to the incident.

The Drive to Achieve

We're too busy, too goal-directed," answered Harvard psychiatrist Edward M. Hallowell when asked why we are rude. In other words, we are rude because, as we run toward our work-related goals, we see no point in slowing down for the sole purpose of being civil. Dr. Hallowell's answer begs the question: "Why are we so busy, so goal-directed?" Well, we certainly need to make ends meet in a challenging work environment, but there is more to it than that. In an anonymous and egalitarian society, we struggle every day to establish our identity and leave our mark.

In traditional hierarchical societies, men and women derived a large amount of their sense of self-worth by belonging to a certain family and/or social class. Pride in "being" was so strong that it made pride in "doing" almost irrelevant. Furthermore, in these societies there were few opportunities to move up the social ladder. Thus motivation to achieve was scant. Whether pride or resigned acceptance was involved in belonging to a family or a social class, individual identity was secure in a way that is irretrievable for us today.

A consequence of the leveling trend of the last several centuries is our increased need to distinguish ourselves through achievement. That we are all equal is a cornerstone of our house of values. Within this frame of mind we are driven to achieve in order to establish our individual identities. We accept that we are equals, but we also want to be different. Thus we scramble; we become "too busy, too goal-directed." As we pull out all the stops in our frenzy of achievement, we often disregard the norms of civility.

Stress

Relentless focus on achievement causes stress. A stressed, fatigued, or distressed person is less inclined to be patient and tolerant, to think before acting, and to be aware of the needs of others. Thus such a person is more likely to be rude. If we manage to lower the stress level in our lives, our everyday encounters with others are less confrontational. But sanity-seeking strategies, like working fewer hours or switching to a job that requires less expenditure of nervous energy, come at a price. Sometimes they entail diminished professional achievement and monetary rewards. Are we willing to seriously consider the trade-off? I hope so, for our own good. And we would be well advised to consider strategies to reduce the stress that comes from other areas of our lives as well. Unfortunately, work is far from being our only stressor.

How We Play the Game

Two related messages surround us wherever we are, 24 hours a day:

- Message A is: You can achieve all that you want. There is no limit to what you can be and do.

- Message B is: What matters in life is to win. The winner is the hero, irrespective of how the win was achieved. Winners take all.

We can all see the merits of message A: it builds self-esteem, it gives hope, and it encourages striving toward worthy goals. It can, however, make us believe that achievement is an absolute value and that it comes before everything else—that goals are important and people don't matter, for instance. Furthermore, it can foster unrealistic expectations. If you are told enough times as a child that you can become the president of the United States or a star professional athlete, you may end up believing that it is *likely* that you will. You may also believe that becoming a good construction worker or a good nurse instead is an unacceptable alternative. The attending disappointment can be crushing.

Message B is even more hazardous for both individuals and society. If winning is the only thing that counts, you may think nothing of crushing others on your way to victory. Then, if you happen to lose you lose everything, your world crumbles around you, and as you vent your frustration you may do serious damage to yourself and others. Think of the vandalism and violence sometimes caused by fans of teams that lost a championship game. Or think of the workplace killings done by people laid off from work.

Suppose that instead we fostered among the young the belief that although it is important to win, how we play the game is even more important. Suppose we convinced them that we play the game well when we play it to the best of our abilities, respecting both the rules of the game and our opponents. Imagine the changes the new frame of mind would bring. Here is a new society where we can lose a game and still be happy with what we did. We might not like the final score, but what really matters, the fact that we played the game well, following our heart and our conscience, cannot be taken away from us. Thus defeat becomes bearable, a learning opportunity rather than a crushing blow. We can easily make our peace with it, leave it behind us, and look forward to our next win. But then, in a way, we are already winners. This is civility: the ability to internalize the notion that how you play the game is more important than the final score.

I wish that the typical confidence-building talk for the young were amended to sound more or less like this: Yes, you may have the potential to achieve all that you want in life. And, yes, you may even become the president of the United States. However, odds are that you won't. You will likely become instead an elementary school teacher, a doctor, a bank teller, a bus driver, a janitor, or the regional manager in a midsize company. These jobs are as respectable as that of president. What really matters is that just as the president does in his or her job, you will have the opportunity in yours to find fulfillment and to change for the better the lives of others.

Two Sides of the Coin

In the last several years new expressions have entered our vocabulary that record some of the least attractive features of the times in which we live. Not only do we have "road rage," but we also have "air rage," the seemingly increasing occurrences of unruly behavior by air travelers, and "desk rage," which is stress-related workplace incivility. Then there is "sports rage," the violent outbursts that parents attending their children's sports games direct at referees and at other parents. Sports rage has become such a concern that parents are sometimes asked to enroll in workshops on civil cheering.

We are being told of an epidemic of bullying in the schools, and we have seen students react to bullying with gunfire. Many Americans think that their schools are responsible for a societal decline in civility that they perceive as getting worse by the day. One of the most disheartening news items at the end of the century was that about the four girls at a Brooklyn, New York, school who beat their sixth-grade teacher for not allowing them to watch *The Jerry Springer Show* on their classroom television set.

Abrasiveness, self-absorption, and just plain rudeness pervade the world of entertainment. Starting in the 1990s, to an unprecedented extent television situation comedies have been defined by their characters' insensitivity. In both radio and television, what a few years ago would have been too coarse, graphic, and irreverent for broadcast is now deemed acceptable for prime time.

Many star professional athletes are known for their abusive aggressiveness, tantrum throwing, and all-around unsportsmanlike conduct. Children imitate them every day on school basketball courts and football fields around the country.

Should this grim picture preoccupy us? Indeed, I think it should. But as I suggested previously, it doesn't necessarily mean that when it comes to basic decency we are living in the worst of times. In fact, depending on where we choose to look, we can argue that we live in times more civil than those gone by. Let me return to and briefly expand on something I observed in part 2.

We live in an age that is much more willing than previous ones to acknowledge the intrinsic value of all members of society, regardless of gender, social provenance, sexual orientation, race, and national origin. We are less likely to react to those who are somehow different from us with hostility, defensiveness, and ridicule. And we are learning to become more inclusive without giving up our principles and our identities.

I remember how odd it seemed to me to see the first women conductors on Italian trains. Now I find it odd—actually, almost incomprehensible—that it should have been so. Women have taken the world of work by storm; they have shown that they can do the job and won't leave the workplace any time soon. There is little doubt in my mind that the number of men who treat women as intellectual and professional peers on the job is much higher today than it was one or two generations ago.

> HIS FATHER HAD HAD A GREAT RESPECT AND LOVE FOR
> WOMEN, HAD DESPERATELY WANTED DAUGHTERS, HAD
> THOUGHT WOMEN CAPABLE OF ANYTHING, SHORT OF AC-
> TIONS REQUIRING GREAT PHYSICAL STRENGTH, THAT A MAN
> CAN DO. BUT HE HAD SEEN THEM, TOO, AS A CIVILIZING
> INFLUENCE WITHOUT WHOSE PECULIAR SENSITIVITY AND
> COMPASSION THE WORLD WOULD HAVE BEEN AN UGLIER
> PLACE.   —*P. D. James*

There is also little doubt that our society has higher standards when it comes to the treatment of its younger members. An impressive number of resources are deployed to improve the intellectual and emotional well-being of the young and the very young. The end result may not always be satisfactory, but the intentions are mostly good.

In general, today's patient enjoys unprecedented respect. Doctors have become better listeners and are not afraid to be kind. They provide their patients with an abundance of information on their conditions and the nature of their illnesses. This helps patients choose with more confidence among therapeutic options. The figure of the brusque medical despot, so common in the Europe of my youth, is on its way to virtual extinction. Still a problem, however, is the physician who doesn't speak, doesn't listen, and does a perfunctory job because of cost-driven time constraints.

Finally, as I observed in Rule 24, we are becoming more careful and loving stewards of the environment and of animals.

What to Do

The end of the twentieth century was a time of extraordinary concern for the state of civility. The media devoted a large amount of attention to the perceived decline in standards of social exchange. I doubt if there ever was another time in which so many civility- and civil-society-oriented initiatives were born and prospered. Among them were the Penn National Commission on Society, Culture and Community and the Johns Hopkins Civility Project. But hundreds of civility committees, civility surveys, civility courses, and civility workshops sprouted up all over the country. Civility Web sites became increasingly popular.

So although it's difficult to deny that recent years have witnessed a coarsening of social interaction in America (at least from a certain point of view), they also witnessed a nationwide effort to bring more respect, decency, consideration, and kindness to the fabric of everyday life. Of course, the two phenomena were connected. The latter was in part a consequence of the former. The fervor of pro-civility initiatives doesn't seem to have abated. It continues in public and private elementary and secondary schools, colleges, business organizations, hospitals, the legal profession, religious communities, and community centers. It is a valiant effort, the crucial necessity for which is becoming more and more apparent in the increasingly diverse communities in which we live.

Today the possibility of cross-cultural misunderstanding and conflict is always present. The more civil the members of society, the less likely for this possibility to become reality. Respect for diversity is part of the cognitive and emotional kit of the civil person, as is the ability to transcend diversity in the name of a common humanity. Will the next generation be able to acquire and practice these two moral skills? Nothing less than our future hangs in the balance.

Angrily contested parking spaces, cellular telephones ringing everywhere, blasting stereos searing the night, offensive anonymous Internet messages, volleys of racial or homophobic epithets in the streets and out-of-control bullying in the schools; shrill fellow air travelers, narcissistic coworkers, yelling supervisors, pushy shoppers, surly salespeople, littering campers, needlessly honking drivers, unsupervised small children disturbing the peace in public places, domineering and snappy stressed-out spouses, and self-serving friends. At the end of the twentieth century we started to have a clear sense that incivility was becoming a problem that couldn't be ignored. We saw a connection between rampant incivility and a diminished quality of life. It is our job now to increase and spread that awareness and make concerted efforts to bring about the changes so many of us seem ready to welcome.

I suggest that we seek ways to

- improve the living conditions and prospects of the poor and the disenfranchised;

- rediscover the teaching of civility and good manners as an invaluable tool to improve everybody's quality of life;

- create opportunities for connection among the members of our communities in order to curb the trend toward more and more anonymity, in other words, revitalizing, civil society; and

- lower the amount of stress in everyday life, especially in the workplace.

Just about the most important thing we do in life is interacting with other human beings. Shouldn't improving the quality of this interaction be at the top of our agendas? Being civil in our everyday lives is a time-tested way to bring about such improvement. A better quality of human interaction makes for a better life—a saner, more meaningful, healthier, and happier life. It is that simple. *It is really that simple.* All we have to do is stop, think about it, and then act. The sooner, the better.

I was on a train on a rainy day. The train was slowing down to pull into a station. For some reason I became intent on watching the raindrops on the window. Two separate drops, pushed by the wind, merged into one for a moment and then divided again—each carrying with it a part of the other. Simply by that momentary touching, neither was what it had been before. And as each one went to touch other raindrops, it shared not only itself, but what it had gleaned from the other. I saw this metaphor many years ago and it is one of my most vivid memories. I realized then that we never touch people so lightly that we do not leave a trace. Our state of being matters to those around us, so we need to become conscious of what we unintentionally share so we can learn to share with intention.

I have read these words by Peggy Tabor Millin many times, but the image of the merging and dividing raindrops doesn't cease to enthrall me. What a vivid and memorable way of clothing a truth both simple and great! "We never touch people so lightly that we do not leave a trace." Millin's words are a quietly insisting murmur resonating in my mind—a gentle murmur of timeless wisdom. What is civility if not a constant awareness that no human encounter is without consequence? What is it if not sharing with intention the best that is in us? Sharing it again and again, adding brightness to the day.

Notes

PART ONE

Life and Relationships

Peter Gadol. This striking paragraph is on page 259 of Gadol's novel *The Long Rain* (New York: St. Martin's Press, Picador, 1998).

M. Scott Peck. Both quotations are from page 15 of *The Road Less Traveled: A New Psychology of Love, Traditional Values and Spiritual Growth* (New York: Simon & Schuster, Touchstone, 1979).

Respect in Action

The principle of respect for persons. This principle entails, according to Errol E. Harris, the following: "First, that each and every person should be regarded as worthy of sympathetic consideration, and should be so treated . . . Secondly, that no person should be regarded by another as a mere possession; or used as a mere instrument, or treated as a mere obstacle, to another's satisfaction; and . . . Thirdly, that persons are not and ought never to be treated in any undertaking as mere expendables." See Errol E. Harris, "Respect for Persons," in *Ethics and Society: Original Essays on Contemporary Moral Problems,* edited by Richard T. De George (London: Macmillan, 1968), p. 113.

Civility does the work of empathy. A solid contribution on empathy is *The Power of Empathy,* by Arthur P. Ciaramicoli and Katherine Ketcham (New York: Penguin, Plume, 2001).

How Do We Learn to Love?

Sigmund Freud. See his *Civilization and Its Discontents* (New York: W. W. Norton, n.d.), pp. 23–24.

Rebecca Wells. The quotation is from page 24 of *Divine Secrets of the Ya-Ya Sisterhood* (New York: HarperCollins, HarperPerennial, 1997).

Civility and Self-Expression

We must forgo fun. On the difference between happiness and fun, see chapter 11 of Dennis Prager's *Happiness Is a Serious Problem: A Human Nature Repair Manual* (New York: HarperCollins, ReganBooks, 1998), pp. 44–52.

Nice Guys Finish Last. Or Do They?

E. M. Forster. The essay is part of the collection *Two Cheers for Democracy* (New York: Harcourt, Brace, 1951). The quotation is from page 73.

The Science of Love and Social Support

Healthy young men. For this study and those that follow, see Dean Ornish, *Love & Survival: The Scientific Basis for the Healing Power of Intimacy* (New York: HarperCollins, 1998), pp. 23–71, and Janice K. Kiecolt-Glaser and others, "Marital Discord and Immunity in Males" in *Psychosomatic Medicine* 50:213–229 (1988). On the connection between relationships and health, see also Brent Q. Hafen and others, *Mind/Body Health: The Effect of Attitudes, Emotions, and Relationships* (Needham Heights: Allyn & Bacon, 1996), Henry Dreher, *The Immune Power Person-*

ality: 7 Traits You Can Develop to Stay Healthy (New York: Plume, 1996), and James J. Lynch, *The Broken Heart: The Medical Consequences of Loneliness* (New York: Basic Books, 1977).

PART TWO: THE RULES

1. Pay Attention

Self-centered obliviousness. This splendid definition is Joshua Halberstam's. See his *Everyday Ethics: Inspired Solutions to Real-Life Dilemmas* (New York: Penguin, 1994), p. 46.

3. Think the Best

The Apostle Paul. See Hebrews 13:2.

4. Listen

Vivian Gussin Paley. The quotations are from *The Kindness of Children* (Cambridge, MA: Harvard University Press, 1999), pp. 63–64.

Open-ended questions. The following passage, from the Ciaramicoli/Ketcham book on empathy, illustrates the difference between open-ended and closed questions: "Suppose Joel comes late to a session. 'We had a disagreement last week,' I say. 'Do you think you might be angry with me and arrived late for our session as a way of letting me know how you felt?' That's a closed question because I have already reached a conclusion (Joel is angry with me). I'm using the question to lead the patient to agree with my interpretation. Here's an example of an open-ended question I might have asked instead. 'I notice that you have been late for the last two sessions, Joel—might this have some meaning we haven't discussed?' That question leaves the answer in the air, unformed. I am truly seeking information and asking the patient to tell me more" (p. 47).

7. Don't Speak Ill

Anonymity . . . just an illusion. See Reed Abelson, "By the Water Cooler in Cyberspace, the Talk Turns Ugly," in the *New York Times*, April 29, 2001, p. 1.

8. Accept and Give Praise

Glenn Van Ekeren. See his book *12 Simple Secrets of Happiness: Finding Joy in Everyday Relationships* (Englewood Cliffs, N.J.: Prentice Hall, 2000), pp. 189–190.

9. Respect Even a Subtle No

ABC News. See ABC News. ABC News Manners Express Poll, May 1999 [Computer file], ICPSR version (Horsham, Penn.: Chilton Research Services [producer], 1999; Ann Arbor, Mich.: Inter-university Consortium for Political and Social Research [distributor], 1999).

11. Mind Your Body

Don't make any noises with your mouth. There are parts of the world where eating noises are expected. They are meant to signify appreciation for the food. See Nadine Dresser, *Multicultural Manners: New Rules of Etiquette for a Changing Society* (New York: John Wiley & Sons, 1996), pp. 74–75.

12. Be Agreeable

Thomas Jefferson. See Jefferson's letter to James Madison of Jan. 30 and Feb. 5, 1787, in *The Republic of Letters: The Correspondence Between Thomas Jefferson and James Madison 1776–1826*, edited by James Morton Smith, vol. 1 (New York: Norton, 1995), p. 461.

13. Keep It Down (and Rediscover Silence)

Les Blomberg. Radio interview with Diane Rehm, WAMU, Washington, D.C., April 24, 2001. I found the motto and the mission of the Noise Pollution Clearinghouse on the home page of the Clearinghouse's Web site (www.nonoise.org). The final quotation comes from an article by Les Blomberg titled "Noise, Sovereignty, and Civility," which can be found in the Online Library of the Clearinghouse's Web site. The article contains an excellent "Good Neighbor Policy," with a wealth of suggestions on how to limit as much as possible the production of noise. Among them: "Rely on silent alarms and devices that disable vehicles to protect cars," "When using a cell phone, move to a private place where you will not disturb others," and "Lay rugs in heavily traveled areas and hallways" if you share walls, floors, or ceilings with others.

15. Respect Other People's Space

The quality of the relationships we have with our coworkers. A study by Prof. Christine Pearson, formerly of the University of North Carolina, gives a sense of the costs attached to incivility in the workplace. Seven hundred and seventy-five workers were asked about rude acts of which they had been the targets. The acts in question were nonphysical violations of the norms of mutual respect. They included: sending a demeaning note, shouting at a coworker, and the public undermining of a coworker's credibility. Twenty-eight percent of the targets of rude acts said that they "lost work time avoiding the instigator"; 53 percent "lost work time worrying about the incident"; 37 percent felt "that their commitment to the organization declined"; 22 percent "decreased their effort at work"; 10 percent "decreased the amount of time that they spent at work"; 46 percent "contemplated changing jobs to avoid the instigator"; 12 percent actually "changed jobs to avoid the instigator" ("Workplace Incivility Is Costly, KFBS Study Says," >www.kenan-flagler@unc.edu< 1999). We may prefer to look at civil behavior as a matter of knowing right from wrong, of knowing that respect for others is simply expected of all of us. Anything affecting the bottom line, however, commands instant attention. Rudeness has tangible costs, we are finally discovering. Will this make a difference?

17. Assert Yourself

Ruth Rendell. The quotation is from page 125 (New York: Dell, 1997).

The three essential elements of a good assertion. Robert Bolton gives an eloquent presentation on the three-part assertion in chapter 9 of his excellent *People Skills: How to Assert Yourself, Listen to Others, and Resolve Conflicts* (New York: Simon & Schuster, Touchstone, 1986), pp. 139–157. On assertion skills, see also his chapters 10 and 11 (pp. 158–202).

The broken record strategy. "The broken record is helpful in dealing with very aggressive or manipulative people who 'won't take no for an answer.' Extremely submissive people who are likely to buy things they don't want from high-pressure salespeople often find this method helpful. It is also useful for those people at the other end of the continuum who are highly aggressive and are apt to lose control and become verbally or even physically abusive. The broken record method can be 100 percent effective in maintaining one's refusal while continuing to retain emotional self-control" (Bolton, p. 197).

Henry Dreher. See chapter 5 of his *The Immune Power Personality: 7 Traits You Can Develop to Stay Healthy* (New York: Plume, Penguin, 1996), pp. 168–210. The quotation is from page 210.

18. Avoid Personal Questions

Judith Martin. See *Miss Manners Rescues Civilization from Sexual Harassment, Frivolous Lawsuits, Dissing, and Other Lapses in Civility* (New York: Crown, 1996), pp. 111–112.

The effort to deal with them as individuals. See Jordan Lite, "Please Ask Me Who, Not 'What,' I Am," in *Newsweek*, July 16, 2001, p. 9.

19. Care for Your Guests

Anthelme Brillat-Savarin. See his *The Physiology of Taste* (Harmondsworth: Penguin, 1994), p. 14.

Dwight Currie. This story is from *How We Behave at the Feast: Reflections on Living in an Age of Plenty* (New York: HarperCollins, Cliff Street Books, 2000), pp. 16–17.

20. Be a Considerate Guest

Jane Austen. I found this delightful quotation from *Emma* in Nigel Rees's *Good Manners: The Complete Guide to Manners and Etiquette in the 1990s*, (London: Bloomsbury, 1994), p. 58.

22. Refrain from Idle Complaints

It spreads your pessimism to them. Research of the past two decades has shown that optimism is good for you. See Martin E. P. Seligman, *Learned Optimism* (New York: Simon & Schuster, Pocket Books, 1992). The following passage from Dr. Seligman's book gives an idea of current views on the advantages of adopting an optimistic outlook: "Life inflicts the same setbacks and tragedies on the optimist as on the pessimist, but the optimist weathers them better . . . The optimist bounces back from defeat, and, with his life somewhat poorer, he picks up and starts again. The pessimist gives up and falls into depression. Because of his resilience, the optimist achieves more at work, at school, and on the playing field. The optimist has better physical health and may even live longer" (p. 208).

Ralph Waldo Emerson. See his *The Conduct of Life*, vol. 6 (Boston Houghton, Mifflin, 1888), p. 188.

24. Respect the Environment and Be Gentle to Animals

Amitai Etzioni. See his *The New Golden Rule: Community and Morality in a Democratic Society* (New York: Basic Books, Perseus Books, 1997), p. 107.

Keep them away from toxic chemicals and plants. The ASPCA has an Animal Poison Control Center. Emergency information is available 24 hours a day by calling (888) 426-4435. I thank Ilona Klein for helping with this rule.

25. Don't Shift Responsibility and Blame

John Ciardi. See Dante Alighieri, *The Inferno* (New York: Mentor, 1982) p. 279.

PART THREE

Striking Through the Form to the Substance

Alexis de Tocqueville. The quotations come from his *Democracy in America*, vol. 2 (New York: Vintage, 1990), pp. 3–4.

The Drive to Achieve

Edward M. Hallowell. See Chris Lee, "An Epidemic of Coarse and Obnoxious Behavior Is in Full Swing. Is There Anything to Be Done?" in *Training,* July 1999, p. 28.

What to Do

Peggy Tabor Millin. The quotation is from her *Mary's Way* (Berkeley, Calif.: Celestial Arts, 1991). I found it in Diane Berke's *The Gentle Smile: Practicing Oneness in Daily Life* (New York: Crossroad, 1995), pp. 78–79.

Suggestions for Further Reading

Anderson, Elijah. *Code of the Street: Decency, Violence, and the Moral Life of the Inner City.* New York: Norton, 1999.

Bolton, Robert. *People Skills: How to Assert Yourself, Listen to Others, and Resolve Conflicts.* New York: Simon & Schuster, Touchstone, 1986.

Brosseau, Jim, ed. *Town and Country Social Graces: Words of Wisdom in a Changing Society,* New York, Hearst, 2002.

Caldwell, Mark. *A Short History of Rudeness: Manners, Morals, and Misbehavior in Modern America.* New York: St. Martin's Press, Picador, 1999.

Carter, Stephen L. *Civility: Manners, Morals, and the Etiquette of Democracy.* New York: Basic Books, 1998.

Dreher, Henry. *The Immune Power Personality: 7 Traits You Can Develop to Stay Healthy.* New York: Plume, Penguin, 1996.

Gallant, Janet. *Simple Courtesies: How to Be a Kind Person in a Rude World.* Pleasantville, N.Y.: Reader's Digest, 1988.

George Washington's Rules of Civility & Decent Behaviour in Company and Conversation. Mount Vernon, Va.: The Mount Vernon Ladies' Association, 1992.

Goleman, Daniel. *Emotional Intelligence.* New York: Bantam, 1997.

Hallowell, Edward M. *Connect.* New York: Pantheon, 1999.

McCullough, Donald. *Say Please, Say Thank You: The Respect We Owe One Another.* New York: G. P. Putnam's Sons, 1998.

Martin, Judith. *Miss Manners Rescues Civilization from Sexual Harassment, Frivolous Lawsuits, Dissing, and Other Lapses in Civility.* New York: Crown, 1996.

Peck, M. Scott. *The Road Less Traveled: A New Psychology of Love, Tradi-*

tional Values and Spiritual Growth. New York: Simon & Schuster, Touchstone, 1979.

Rouner, Leroy S., ed. *Civility.* Notre Dame, Ind.: University of Notre Dame Press, 2000.

Van Ekeren, Glenn. *12 Simple Secrets of Happiness: Finding Joy in Everyday Relationships.* Englewood Cliffs, N.J.: Prentice Hall, 2000.

Williams, Lena. *It's the Little Things: The Everyday Interactions That Get Under the Skin of Blacks and Whites.* New York: Harcourt, 2000.

Williams, Virginia, and Redford Williams. *Lifeskills: Eight Simple Ways to Build Stronger Relationships, Communicate More Clearly, and Improve Your Health.* New York: Times Books, Random House, 1998.